The Most Important Conversation Is the One *You're Not Having*

by

Susan E. Greene

The Most Important Conversation
Is the One You're Not Having

by

Susan E. Greene

Copyright 2003
Susan E. Greene
(revised edition)

Cover design
Joan R. Neubauer

ISBN 1-932196-10-2

Word Wright International
P.O. Box 1785
Georgetown, Texas

Printed in the United States of America

Kudos for Susan E. Greene

"Congratulations on creating a gift that I know will be helpful and meaningful. The wonderful content fuels conversation and change that will bless many."

Reverend Howard Caesar
Unity Church of Christianity

"Congratulatons! Our Speaker Recognition Program honors and acknowledges you for achieving specified high levels of tenure, content and delivery combined. Thank you for the substantial influence you've had in increasing effectiveness and enhancing the lives of CEOs."

The Speaker Development Department
TEC, an International Organization of CEOs

Sampson, I dedicate this book to you. You have been my teacher since you arrived February 19,1990. You have taught me the joy of being in the moment. You look me straight in the eyes and see my truth. Being your mother I've learned to be self-disciplined and diligently "walk my talk" in all my relationships. Without you I would not know unconditional love, total acceptance and complete trust.

I love you.

Mom.

Table of Contents

Acknowledgements

I wish to thank all of you who have read my drafts, helped me edit and blessed me with your encouragement. Joan thank you for helping me make this a reality.

Dad, I am "greatfull" to you for teaching me the value of integrity, and I will always remember how you loved me unconditionally. Mom, you taught me that people are all the same. "We put our pants on one leg at a time." You modeled the importance of being a servant-leader to make a difference in other people's lives.

Katie, you have more strength and love than most of us can even imagine let alone demonstrate. And to my nephew, Matt, for loving yourself enough, thank you.

To all the loving people who have supported me on this journey I am "greatfull." Linda, you have always been there. Dana, your love and support have no boundaries. Sue, you are my vision keeper. Thank you.

Eileen, special thanks for collaborating and sharing ideas, processes and thoughts about how to help others be in control of their emotions. You will see your contribution to my work in this book as I see mine in yours. We have shared so much about our work that sometimes I can't even remember who came up with the idea first. Thank you for sharing the journey.

Calene, you taught me the value of receiving. Merlyn, you gave me my first large contract. Then you became my very dear friend. Gary, you're showing me how to let go of judgment. Trish, thank you for calling me "earth angel." Margaret, you always listened.

Anke, your coaching has helped me grow and remember my own strength through the very difficult times. Les Murray, you said, "Whatever you love to do, someone is doing it and getting paid." I heard the word "passion" when you said love. I found my passion in my work that has become my "calling" since 1986. Thank you.

Neal, you taught me how to reach my anger. More importantly, without you, Sam wouldn't be here to bless our lives. Thank you for being a great father.

To my extended family, I appreciate your love. Being with you is so much fun and when we're all together I love the laughter. To all my friends who have helped me know and understand loving relationships. Thank you.

Dr. Kathryn Kotrla, you endorsed my process and helped me see the true value in sharing it. Jeff Clarke and Lisa Yoram, you believed in my potential. Michael and Arni Berry, for incredible trust. Carla Cooper for expanding my horizons. Dr. John Younker for challenging me to create this process for TEC. Thank you.

Those of you who come for coaching and give me the privilege to listen to the intimate details of your life, I will always feel honored. All of you, who have sat in my sessions or listened to me on television, thank you.

For those of you in TEC who have opened up and shared your challenges with me in front of your peers, words cannot express how I've treasured each of those moments.

Without you there would be no book. Thank you, for blessing my life.

Jim, you've helped me grow, expand, heal and feel safe. Your acknowledgement of my gifts and talents is very precious. Thank you for being and sharing my life as partner, husband, lover and friend. *You nurture my soul.*

Introduction

"The most important conversation in any organization is the one you are not having. You all know what it is. What would happen if you had it?"

—*Rick Eigenbrod*

"The driving social issue in any community is the issue no one is willing to talk about."

—*Ivan Browning*

Why this book? What can Susan Greene tell you that you haven't heard before?

PBS Houston Public Television calls Susan Greene the Communication Expert. Her clients know her as a CEO, consultant, professional speaker, master facilitator, coach, author, television personality, friend, "shrink" and an angel. Susan calls herself a catalyst, mother, sister, friend and mentor.

In 1999, The Executive Committee Worldwide (TEC) asked Susan to teach the CEO members in roundtables of eight to 17 participants how to confront each other on their very tough issues. This is the process she developed for TEC.

Since then, she has coached over 600 CEOs as well as her clients on the Power of Candor throughout the United States and Canada. Here is the process. Here are the stories these

CEOs and other clients want to share with you on how they learned the power of candor. Their stories are true. The names and organizations have been changed or omitted to respect their privacy.

Why is Susan Greene qualified to write this book? Over and over again her clients have asked, "Where is your book?"

Greene's clients continue to tell Susan that her approach is different. They learn how to have difficult conversations effectively that honors both parties. They now understand what drives anger and frustration, more importantly, how to handle it quickly.

Many of those responses motivated Susan to clear her schedule, sit down and capture it on paper.

"Your presentation and process was fantastic. Your knowledge, walking the talk and obvious inner peace shows through and makes your presentation more meaningful. You are doing good works and helping people immensely."
—D. Palmer, CEO, District of Columbia

"Whatever my husband was released from was something that I knew nothing about and all I can say is thank you. He is less angry having more fun and calmer now when he comes home from work. He certainly has experienced something profound."
—A. Hodge, Wife of a client, Ontario, Canada

"As I reflect on the past year the best value my CEO group received was from you. There is a great need for your insightful thoughts. You 'compellingly' communicate imaginative ideas very well. You ARE making a difference."
—C. Ferneyhough III, TEC Chair, Virginia

"I felt like I really connected with you. You are very skilled and knowledgeable about your topic and the result is you are effective. I am sure that many people share my feelings about you and the benefits that have resulted in their lives."
                              —A. Whiting, CEO, New Hampshire

"I've been in anger management for two years. I got in touch with my feelings and all that stuff. Today, the light bulb went off. I now know how to fix it. I can do this now. Thank you for showing me HOW!"
                              —J. Post, California

"Your lovely spirit and wonderful teachings have come to my rescue more than once. I am lucky to know you."
                              —T. Avery, Union President, Texas

"After the executive and board retreats in Round Top, we are building a foundation on rock, instead of sand. We know our vision. For our next retreat, continue to do what you do well, take the management team 'out of the box'. We are ready to go to our next level."
                              —B. Osterhout, CEO/Chairman, Texas

"Thank you! I still carry the touchstone, and it works for me. Much better, and deeper conversations. You've something there. How are you going to 'fill up the whole world with it'?" D. Morris, CEO, New Jersey

You may not have the opportunity to work directly with Susan. If not you can learn about these ideas, tools and how to use them in this book, *The Most Important Conversation Is the One You're Not Having.*

If you have already worked with Susan, besides this book being a quick refresher for you, she's included many stories and a few more insights. Here's another opportunity to expand your capacity to be candid in all situations.

Just before going to print Susan received this email. We decided to share it with you.

Your visit (obviously not coincidental!) was timely as I knew that my colleague/friend of over 20 years who I had just hired, had gotten off on the wrong foot. He misunderstood his role in the company. We discovered this the evening before your session, Power of Candor. I was deeply troubled that his departure from the company was most certainly necessary. Not only because of the loss of friendship it would entail, but because I knew he could do the job we had hired him for and it would be a loss to the company as well.

Two days after your session we had a conversation about the entire issue. Focusing on the principals of the "Power of Candor," we had a great and open conversation. I emphasized how I was feeling about the entire incident. I explained how I saw his role in the organization now and in the future. Then he opened up about his feelings, fears and observations.

When our conversation ended we both clearly understood (in a non-threatening way), that he needed to embrace the position he was hired for or leave the company. He said, "I am staying and am enthusiastic about my role here."

Now, several weeks later, he has proven that he can do the position intended. He can generate enthusiasm and has regained the respect from the staff. It's amazing what we can do as company leaders when we become human and show by example how others can safely do the same.

The result is that I saved a friendship. My firm has a skilled and dedicated employee. He is happy and committed to our strategic plan and clearly sees a future for himself. Without the "Power of Candor," everyone would have lost— me, my friend, my colleague and my company. With it we all have won. "The Power of Candor" is truly powerful, thank you.

Personal Note from the Author

My seminar, "The Power of Candor" and this book, *The Most Important Conversation Is the One You're Not Having* are about having difficult conversations with you, family, co-workers, friends and others. The tools discussed within this book create the safety to conduct these tough conversations in the "heat of the moment" when you don't have time to prepare.

Do you really have the time to wait? Meanwhile you have given away your power until you deal with the situation. Here among these pages you'll discover proven tools that enable you to manage your anger and have the conversation *now*. Don't put it off.

In Chapter One, we'll cover the triggers that undermine our relationships: passive aggressive, aggressive and passive behaviors. You will learn how these inappropriate behaviors keep you from creating healthy, responsible relationships.

Irritations and frustrations create stress in the body. You will become more aware of their effect on your health. In chapter two you will learn what choices make a significant impact on your body and relationships.

What are the undesirable actions and behaviors in your organization and in your home? Discover in chapter three what are the causes. How can you change them?

In Chapter Four, we will explore brain science and how it affects our behavior. Have you ever said, "I'm so upset, I can't think straight!" Learn why this is true based on how the brain functions.

After a full day of meetings you come home tired from work, whereas 60 minutes of physical exercise energizes you. In chapter five, we'll demonstrate how and why this phenomenon happens time and again.

"USA Today" July 18, 2000 read, "Our lives are all crumpled up with stress, multi-tasking, high expectations, lack of manners. Now we are amid a new epidemic of anger – sometimes deadly anger." Anger, rage and hostility are secondary emotions. What drives us to the point of anger? How do we *fix it*? The answers are in Chapter Six.

Dr. Kathryn Kotrla is board certified by the American Board of Psychiatry & Neurology. Kotrla is head of Psychiatry at Baylor College of Medicine. She has endorsed these techniques on the PBS production, "Brain at Work," as effective ways to handle emotions. The tool, *"Report Report Report"* can be used during any situation or conversation when it gets sticky. In chapter seven you will learn this valuable reporting tool that has helped thousands of people.

When you find yourself in struggle, you are caught in a short circuit that continues to repeat over and over again. Together in Chapter Eight we will explore how giving up incessant addictive thinking patterns takes you out of struggle and into peace.

Chapter Nine is about making choices that are important to you that profoundly impact your life.

The media is consumed with the conversation around terrorism. In 1974, I missed being a bomb casualty by 60 seconds. In Chapter Ten learn how I handled daily terrorist activities in Europe where I worked. Do the exercises that will help you develop a new awareness that will keep you safe.

Since the first edition of this book I've found deeper feelings of joy and peace. In Chapter Eleven I share how living in the question brings answers from God. This has changed my life. How does it get any better than this?

Life is a continuing journey and so is my work. I continue to recreate my material and teaching methods. If you need more clarification or help regarding any of these concepts, please contact me through the website: http://communicatingworks.com

Many of these concepts will challenge your belief systems. I invite you to disengage from your present beliefs allowing you to temporarily let go of your thoughts about reality. When you go to the movies you immerse yourself into the story on the screen, you are not focused on reality.

In reading *The Most Important Conversation Is the One You're Not Having*, disband your present beliefs and judgments until the end of the book. Allow yourself to embrace these new ideas. When you finish reading, choose what is appropriate and works for you. Let go of the rest.

Chapter One

Triggers that Undermine Effectiveness

"To be happy at home is the ultimate result of all ambition." —*Samuel Johnson*

When frustrated or irritated, you interact and communicate in one of three behaviors: passive aggressive, aggressive or passive. All three compromise your effectiveness in managing conflict or dealing with a problem.

Passive Aggressive Behavior

Our society today challenges us in the extreme because our humor tends to be passive aggressive. We have forgotten how to be funny without it being at the expense of someone else.

Turn on the television. Go to the movies. The screens are filled with examples of passive aggressive behavior. The number one culprit is sarcasm. This has challenged many of the CEOs I've worked with over the past year.

Many like sarcasm. They banter with their buddies in the office and on the golf course. They offer sarcasm in large helpings at home around the dinner table.

Several years ago a senior executive at a Fortune 100 company challenged me during our first session. Extremely obnoxious, everyone else tended to "tip toe" around his antics.

What I saw was not an obnoxious man, but a scared man. He had the letters F-E-A-R etched across his forehead. The next day when we had a couple minutes of privacy, I asked him what he was afraid of. Quite surprised by my question he pondered it and started to open up.

After two more retreats with this executive group, we had developed a trusting relationship. He asked me to lead a five-day retreat with his executive team. During that session he faced his biggest obstacle as a leader. For the first time he willingly looked at his truth.

He sat in a chair at the front of the room. Each of his executives told him about a time he/she felt confused or distrust as a result of his sarcasm. He was sure his five bantering buddies wouldn't remember any situations. But they did.

By the time the 26th person spoke, he gave the game up. It took tremendous courage to listen and absorb what he heard that day. That was on Thursday. Friday his daughter arrived home from college with her boyfriend to meet the family. Here's his story.

Waking up Monday morning, thinking about the weekend with his daughter, he had the sudden awareness that he greeted his possible future son-in-law to the family by being sarcastic all weekend!

Immediately he picked up the phone and called her in Philadelphia. "Sara, this is Dad. Please forgive me. Recently I discovered that my sarcastic manner is not the way I choose to welcome David into our family. Your mother and I will fly to Phiily this weekend to reintroduce us. This time, no sarcasm."

He called me that Monday morning to say, "Susan, I got it. Not an easy journey, but it has been well worth it. Thank you for not giving up on me."

After working with thousands of people, I have learned that close inspection reveals that sarcasm creates confusion. What did they really mean?

Sarcasm

Sarcasm has a double meaning. The brain doesn't know where to put the information. I pulled up the word "sarcasm" from the dictionary on the Web.

> **Sarcasm (noun)**
> **French sarcasme, from Late Latin sarcasmos, from Greek sarkasmos; to tear flesh, bite the lips in rage. First appeared in 1550, a sharp and often satirical utterance designed to cut or give pain**

For example, John always arrives late for meetings. When he walks in the door 30 minutes late you smile and say, "Thanks for being on time, John."

John sees you smile. He hears your thanks. Your voice sounds pleasant, but he knows he's late.

It's a confusing message. Your ***voice, facial expression, and words are not congruent with the situation***.

In a meeting working on a new project, Sally is upset because her boss insists she works late three nights this week for no additional pay. She has an idea that would benefit the project, but feels the company isn't treating her well. She decides to **withhold valuable information**.

Jim wasn't selected for a promotion he felt he deserved yet is asked to train the new person, Tom, on how to use a particular piece of equipment. Jim chooses not to give Tom all the details. He *set* Tom *up to fail*.

Sherry feels she isn't pretty. Her sister, Jill is really cute. Dad gives Jill much more attention. Sherry is often making **unkind** and **demeaning remarks** to Jill. She likes to **put** her **down** and make her cry. When Jill's eyes are puffy and red she's not very cute.

Another example of passive aggressive behavior occurs with Mack. His job is mowing the lawn. On Sunday at 4:00 PM he finally gets out to do the job after much prodding. Feeling resentful, Mack mows the lawn but not the edging. It is an **incomplete job**.

All these types of passive aggressive behavior create conflict and erode relationships. Often the victim of the passive aggression laughs because he does not know how to respond. The laughter lightens the moment.

Confusion remains behind. What did they really mean? What did they want from me? Why me? Trust in the relationship diminishes.

At work you may think trust isn't important. That person just works here. Harvard Business School did a case study at Bell Labs several years ago attempting to understand the superstars. They discovered trust does count.

They observed a team of 150 engineers. All had similar credentials both in education and technical skills. The top 10% continued to out perform the others. Why?

These superstars solved problems quicker than the others.

How did they do that if they had the same degrees and technical expertise?

The superstars spent their time building trusting relationships. When they called or e-mailed a colleague to get assistance on a problem, they found that even though they were the 11th message, it was the first call to be returned. Based on the relationship, the problem became the top priority.

Living in a global economy that never sleeps and constantly inundates us with information, how do we have enough time with our family and ourselves? On top of that I'm suggesting that you develop deeper relationships with your colleagues. If you want help quickly, when you need it, remember friends help friends.

Aggressive Behavior

Aggressive behavior is easier to recognize than passive aggressive behavior. Examples include *loud voices, tempers, cursing, bullying, fighting, slamming doors* and *telephones* as well as *throwing objects*.

Interactions are *dictatorial, direct, controlling* and "in your face." Aggressive people think that they must control others and tell them what to do in order to get results. Most people react to their orders. They also don't feel appreciated and heard.

In every human resource survey I've seen during the past two decades, respect, appreciation and being listened to rank higher than money if you earn more than minimum wage.

Tom was the first Regional Manager of a large organization willing to hire the first saleswoman in their industry back in 1977.

After 16 weeks training at headquarters and touring the USA plants of all their suppliers and manufacturing plants, I started working in the regional offices.

The first week on the job, I went to Dallas to meet customers. On Friday when I called my office, my boss started screaming on the phone.

"Whatever happened to that freight car that shipped all our product back to the plant? What are you doing about it?" He kept yelling at me about a client I wasn't even told was mine yet.

I soon discovered their volume potential warranted only one sales call a year.

Dismayed by my treatment, I asked if Tom would meet me in his office at 8:00 AM Monday morning.

Monday I went into his office and shut the door. I said, "Tom, I know this is only my second week on the job after training. It will take a few days to learn who are my clients and about their issues, but I choose to be treated as a professional, regardless of the problems. If I need to correct something or work with a client to solve a problem, I'll do it. My father never yelled at me, and I don't choose to work in an environment where I'm treated this way. Would you like me to resign now or can we work together in another way?"

As you can well imagine, a young woman had never questioned him before. Tom took a deep breath and said, "don't leave."

From that moment on he treated me with respect and we became good friends. Six months later during a reception at headquarters the president surprised me.

"I hear you've tamed Tom. He hasn't yelled at anyone since you joined his team. Tom is a great manager but he was constantly intimidating the women in the plant and the offices. No one has burst into tears since you arrived. Thanks."

Much later when I left the company, I received the usual farewell gift. Tom also gave me a very special personal gift. The gift wasn't what was special, it was what he said when he gave it. "Thank you for teaching me how to work with my anger and treat people better. What I taught you here was so little in comparison to the gifts you've given me."

Passive Behavior

Passive behavior is commonplace in our organizations and in our homes. In my family we were passive. When my parents announced they were divorced, my sister and I were shocked. They never fought. There were no arguments in our house except the usual sibling rivalry. What we experienced was the *silent treatment*. The problems were *ignored* and *denied*.

The issues I see too often in companies are the challenges that are created by the people who have the *"need to please disease."* They avoid conflict at all costs.

Whenever these friendly people are asked to do something they say "yes." They are *afraid to say "no"* which may lead to conflict.

Tasks and projects begin to pile up and they go into overwhelm. They miss deadlines and do not handle priorities well.

Richard, CEO of a television station is well liked by his people. Whoever he asks to do something usually wants to please him regardless of the urgency of the project they may already have at the time.

7

Richard learned in delegating tasks to ask what were their priorities. Were they working on preparing a live show to be aired that day? If so, he needed to find someone else to handle the task.

You know these passive people in your organizations. They are friendly, hard working and constantly juggling too many tasks at once. Before you give them another project, you may help them renegotiate their priorities.

These three behaviors, passive aggressive, aggressive and passive all erode relationships. At different times we all have probably experienced these three behaviors. The key is to learn appropriate and responsible behavior.

At http://www.communicatingworks.com you'll find the *free* **Interaction Quotient Quiz**. This do-it-yourself online quiz takes just a few minutes. Invite all your friends, co-workers and family to take the IQ Quiz. You may find the results very interesting.

A vice president of a Fortune 100 company sent this after I conducted their executive retreat:

I have seen stronger willingness to address the tougher issues head-on and confront stressful situations with more accountability. I have witnessed greater effort by the passives (including me), to face the aggressives and not let them steam-roll over others.

I believe the benefit from this is people are taking more control over their destiny by providing alternatives, ideas and solutions. In the past they would sit back and let it roll by with no input.

Accountability for our actions and communications creates healthy responsible relationships we can depend on.

We maintain respect and trust grows. In *Difficult Conversations* by Stone, Patton and Heen write, *"Have your feelings or they will have you."*

Being responsible means maintaining control. Control your feelings. Control your words. Control your actions. It does not mean control other people's feelings, words and actions. Stop the drama. Speak from the heart. Don't stuff your feelings or project them outwards through anger or barbs.

In this communication-intensive time, the breakthroughs for both individuals and organizations are internal.

Self-aware people don't resist change; they don't make counter productive decisions based on feelings they don't even realize they have.

People who know what drives them are much more willing to take risks, test new ideas, and aggressively pursue opportunities.

The knowledge they gain gives them an advantage that can no longer be gained through external means.

--Morris Shechtman

Exercise

Everyone at some time in their life has acted out a few of these different behavior aspects when irritated, angry or challenged. Circle the behavior that you experience most often when you're upset.

Passive aggressive
- Mismatch of facial expression, tone of voice and words
- Sarcasm that is personal
- Put down
- Revenge
- Setting others up for failure
- Withholding information
- Resentment

Aggressive
- Loud voices
- Temper
- Throwing objects
- Bullying
- Cursing

Passive
- Silent treatment
- Ignoring
- Denial
- Seething
- Saying "yes" when you want to say "no"

Notes

Rapid Recall

> ➤ How can you use these concepts and tools in this chapter?

> ➤ What can you do differently?

> ➤ What steps are you willing to take, starting now, to put this into action?

> ➤ What will happen if you do this for 30 days?

> ➤ How will your life change?

Notes

Chapter Two

Body Beware

"It's terribly amusing how many different climates of feeling one can go through in a day."

— *Anne Morrow Lindbergh*

During the day people get their buttons pushed. Many of you find yourself irritated, frustrated or challenged by co-workers, family or even the traffic.

Preparing for my sessions with CEOs, I ask them to keep notes on all the many things that push their buttons during the day. It only takes a few minutes to reflect on the past 24 hours.

You will develop a deeper awareness of your emotions if you do this exercise for a minimum of one week. Keep these notes for 30 days. It will be an eye opener.

Right now, let us focus on the past few days. What irritates you?

For example, a driver suddenly pulled in front of you while you were waiting in line to enter the freeway. Or the woman in the express lane (six items or less) at the grocery store had 12 items and coupons. Maybe last night after your son's bedtime, he finally announced he needed red construction paper from Target for a project at school in the morning.

Look at the things that frustrate you. Which is the most challenging one? Maybe it is road rage. Sit quietly for a moment. Recall this irritating incident and how annoyed you were. Scan your whole body to discover where the tension resonates.

Whenever you get annoyed, frustrated, irritated or angry, the brain releases stress hormones. Tension will resonate somewhere in the body. The examples clients have told me are: racing heart, face flushes, clenched hands, sweating palms, headache, shoulder tension, back pain, neck pain, pain behind the eyes, whole body tension, nausea, tight gut, tension in the chest, perspiration, tight throat, voice change, heavy sigh, shaking leg while sitting and talking, fidgeting, clenched jaw.

Dr. Price, a dentist said, "grinding teeth at night is evidence you are stressed and clench your jaw during the day."

Any of these body responses familiar? Most people experience one or two of these on a regular basis.

Exercise

Write down the behaviors and actions that irritate you i.e. road rage, being late to a meeting or kept waiting in the doctor's office.

➤ Use the next page as a chart for this exercise.

➤ In the left column, write down five things that irritate, frustrate or make you angry. Use the notes you've taken over the past month or think of new ones.

➤ In the right column, write down the corresponding stimuli you feel in your body. Examples: tight throat, sick stomach, headache, back hurts, clenched hands, heart racing, face flushed, sweating, clenched jaw, etc.

➤ Look over what you wrote down. Are any of these irritants *big stuff*?

Actions/Behaviors	Where in the Body

What's the Big Stuff?

A wonderful friend used to tell his wife, "Rosie, don't sweat the small stuff."

She got so annoyed one day and asked, "Okay, what is the BIG stuff?"

He responded, "Rosie, the BIG stuff is when you are born and when you die. All the stuff in between is small stuff."

What we learn from medical science is stress accumulates over a period of time and creates stress related disease. While preparing the PBS television production of "Brain at Work," Saurage-Thibodeaux Research (http://www.saurage-research.com) reported that the U.S. drug prescription market for 1998 totaled $92.14 billion. The top four drugs were for stress related diseases.

The Gulfstar Group, Inc. reported that the worldwide market for antidepressants for 1999 reached $10.8 billion. They project sales will reach $20.7 billion in year 2005.

Many of you reading this are part of these statistics. Thank you for getting a copy of this book. Congratulate yourself for continuing to look for ways to get a handle on your stress. There are a number of proven tools in this book. Keep reading and take the time to do all the exercises.

Many people don't take a prescribed drug, they self-medicate in other ways. I would crave comfort foods like, pasta, ice cream or cookies when I wasn't willing to talk about a problem. I'd stuff down my feelings as well as my food.

Some people over exercise and keep the adrenaline highs running for long periods of time. Others drink too much caffeine or alcohol. Maybe you gave up cigarettes, but now you smoke cigars.

Neale Donald Walsch wrote in *Conversations with God* about two ways to commit suicide. Quick suicide is when you point a gun at your head and pull the trigger. Slow suicide is when you consciously participate daily in activities that create dis-ease.

Emotional Intelligence

Dr. Daniel Goleman gave us a new way to talk about emotions when he wrote *Emotional Intelligence* and *Working with Emotional Intelligence. Webster's Dictionary* defines intelligence as the ability to learn and understand.

In our society we usually refer to intelligence in terms of learning and understanding facts and situations. Emotional Intelligence, or EQ, is how we learn and understand our emotions.

My mother was bright, intellectual, interesting and very active. Although she never held a salaried job, she contributed to her community in powerful ways.

One winter I remember my parents parked their cars outside in the snow because Girl Scout cookies completely filled the garage. Mom was the Girl Scout Cookie Chairman for Ulster County.

Back in the 50s, Mom created quite a stir as President of the PTA when she brought Eleanor Roosevelt to Woodstock, New York to address our small community about the children in Russia. Later she was elected to the School Board.

By the time I reached high school, she changed her focus. She chaired the fund raising project that built the first public hospital in the U.S. with only private sector funds. In 1966, it attracted so much attention that First Lady Byrd Johnson came for the opening ceremonies.

All the leadership qualities and energy my mother had serving the community, she never developed emotional intelligence. She stuffed her anger. No one ever saw my mother, Janet, without a pleasant smile, regardless of how she felt.

Just before heart surgery, Mom told my friend Vicki she wished she had quit smoking. Otherwise she treated her body well. Living in the Caribbean, most mornings after her one-mile swim, she snorkeled and went shelling. She ate a heart healthy diet by today's standards.

Janet died at the age of 49 from heart disease.

At her funeral her best friend sadly told me, "I loved your mother. You know how close we were, but she never would share with me her pain."

Heart Disease #1 Killer

Did you know that heart disease is the number one killer in America? More people die of heart disease than cancer and AIDS combined every year according to the American Heart Association.

In a conversation in spring 2000 with the famous Dr. Denton Cooley, head of Texas Heart Institute, he told me of his concern that today men as young as 30 are having heart attacks. He also said that more women than men die of heart disease.

Dr. Brenda Davies, Director of Acute Services in London, England told me women usually don't incur problems until they're menopausal because estrogen is a great protector. Most women go undetected for years because symptoms are not necessarily related to pain around the heart area. The symptoms can be headaches and indigestion that doctors often believe just indicates stress.

According to Dr. Davies, directing your frustration and anger inward does just as much damage to the body as directing it outward, aggressively or passive aggressively. One of the most powerful ways to protect yourself from heart disease is handle your emotions in responsible, healthy ways.

Rapid Recall

> ➤ How can you use these concepts and tools in this chapter?

> ➤ What can you do differently?

> ➤ What steps are you willing to take, starting now, to put this into action?

> ➤ What will happen if you do this for 30 days?

> ➤ How will your life change?

Notes

Chapter Three

Model of Success

"Men are disturbed not by things that happen, but by their opinions of the things that happen."

—*Epictetus*

The model of success in any organization is the CEO/president. I wrote this chapter for those of you leading groups of people as the president or a manager. If you aren't managing or leading a group, you may choose to skip this chapter. Although at some time in your life you will likely lead a group, such as the Boy Scouts, or a Little League team.

Action and behavior is the effect or evidence of a stimulus. Someone knocks on the door (stimulus). Your dog barks (action). Let's look at the undesirable behaviors and stimuli in your life.

What are some examples of undesirable behaviors in your organization or group? Look back at your notes in chapter two. You'll already have some listed.

These examples came from a recent group of CEOs:

> ➢ *Won't speak up*
> ➢ *What's in it for me*
> ➢ *Not my job*
> ➢ *Late to meetings*

- *Lack of accountability*
- *Apathy*
- *One up-man-ship*
- *Lack of initiative*
- *Blame*
- *Put downs*
- *Withholding information*
- *Sarcasm*
- *Excuses*
- *Tempers*
- *Missed appointments*
- *No cooperation*
- *Setting people up*
- *Negative attitude*
- *Gossip*
- *Missed deadlines*

As the CEO or senior executive, you provide the model of success. Ted is president of ABC Corporation and as such is the model of success at ABC Corporation. Jane as Managing Director of DEF Company is the model for success at DEF Company. Jane is not the success model for ABC Corporation, nor is Ted the success model for DEF Company.

One of my Texas clients, Michael, was challenged by how he defined his success early in his career.

Sam, the new Director of Worldwide Operations, promoted Michael to his first CEO position. Sam had been with the company for 20+ years. Starting from engineering support, Sam had a thorough knowledge of the company. People depended upon him for answers. The culture of the company was just that, go to Sam and ask his opinion. The phrase in the company was, "Sam says…."

At first, Michael tried to emulate Sam, but quickly learned that he did not have the experience or knowledge. Michael's key people in the organization did, though most of them didn't realize it. How could he bring this out?

Working with Michael, I helped him see what it took to be a powerful servant-leader.

Michael says, "With my executive committee (EXCOM), I allowed myself to be vulnerable by admitting that I did not have all of the answers. We did as a group. This simple statement opened a new door for the EXCOM and me. They realized that they could make decisions and mistakes. While they would be held accountable, it was not the end of the world. Only the end of the 'Sam says…era' for the first time, they were in control."

Michael learned that was only the beginning.

"During my eight years as president/CEO, I mentored, grew and promoted the EXCOM members. The complexion of the group changed many times. The EXCOM members were based on the talent of the individual and what they could bring to the table, not their position. My focus was to help people become the best they could be. To encourage growth in their current position and prepare them for their next challenge. This process was actually a blessing in disguise. The continuous 'new blood' created tremendous innovation and profits during a difficult market.

"What did I learn? Surround yourself with talented people and focus on their growth. Let them know you don't have all the answers, they do. Give people permission to make mistakes. Model being accountable. It will take the organization to success beyond all expectations."

If you are the success model in your organization, what undesirable behaviors do you model? What behaviors do you solicit? How many inappropriate actions do you enable because you continue to allow them to take place? Most CEOs fear that someday people will find out they do not have all the answers. They are afraid to be seen as a weak leader.

One CEO in New York shared with me that although he has all the trappings and wealth of success, he still feels like the inexperienced young man he was when he first started his career.

This is a time to be brutally honest with you. You are the stimulus. What undesirable actions and behaviors do you model, solicit or enable? How many do you have? Take a few minutes to ponder how you create these situations. What are you willing to do about them?

Morris Shechtman has written a great book I highly recommend, *The Internal Frontier*.

He says we are in a communication intensive time, where breakthroughs for both individuals and organizations are internal. People who are self-aware don't resist change nor make productive decisions based on feelings they don't even have. They know what drives them. Much more willing to take risks, test new ideas, and aggressively pursue opportunities. "The knowledge they gain gives them an advantage that can no longer be gained through external means."

A couple weeks after presenting to a group of CEOs I received this email:

"I took several pages of notes and have re-read them almost daily. For most of my life, I have rigorously developed my intellect at the expense of emotional development. As a result, I am instinctively suspicious of anyone and anything

which 'moves me,' 'touches my heart', etc.

"Candor is probably the purest form of truth and we use it selectively, especially with ourselves. First, I found it difficult to be candid with myself. I forced myself to ask this question, 'What are my major self-deceptions?' While struggling to answer that question, I then felt forced to ask another. 'How have these self-deceptions complicated my relationships with others?'

"Therefore, because candor is by its nature the result of a rational process, I am very comfortable with being candid intellectually (e.g. facing the facts, cutting through the crap)...but I suspect that's not 'where it's at.' I now struggle with words to describe what probably defies description. You've given me a great deal to think about. However long it takes, I will attempt to reconnect with emotions that have been neglected (but not denied) for decades. Therein lies the great value of candor."

Exercise

Actions and behaviors are the effect or evidence from a stimulus.

> ➢ What are some examples of undesirable behaviors in your organization, group or family?

> ➢ What triggers these behaviors?

> ➢ Take a minute and look over this list. Do you **solicit, enable** or **model** any of these behaviors? *What's important is for you being aware of how you trigger different behaviors within your organization, group or family.*

> ➢ What steps can you take now to change your behavior and actions?

Rapid Recall

➢ How can you use these concepts and tools in this chapter?

➢ What can you do differently?

➢ What steps are you willing to take, starting now, to put this into action?

➢ What will happen if you do this for 30 days?

➢ How will your life change?

Notes

31

Chapter Four

The Brain

"I have great hope for tomorrow. My hope lies in the following three things: Truth, youth and love."
— *Buckminster Fuller*

To understand the role of the brain in managing conflict and solving problems let us look at two of the many systems within the brain: limbic and cortex.

Emotional Brain – Limbic System

The limbic system is the emotional brain or sometimes referred to as the primitive brain center. Some neurologists refer to it as the reptilian or the "old" brain. This system controls our survival and emotional needs and is fully developed at birth.

The limbic system initiates the triggers to take action when we have concerns about being hurt, safe, jealous, angry, vengeful, blame, impulsive, threatened, guilty, shamed, regret, or fearful.

The emotional brain also controls our needs and desires. It triggers the survival instinct for the fight or flight response. The limbic center controls the physical emotional feelings that make us take action. It also thrives on predictable, routine and familiar patterns.

A baby has a fully developed limbic system. When a baby feels hungry, cold, wet, scared or lonely, which are all survival needs, the limbic system responds to the emotional need by triggering the baby to cry.

Babies and children thrive on routine, the predictable and the familiar because the limbic system has predominant control.

Adaptability

As human beings, we find comfort with the predictable. Morris Shechtman calls it the "familiar." In chapter eight I talk about the familiar being our "story."

Always needing to live in a comfortable predictable world creates incredible challenges. As you no doubt have noticed, our environment is rapidly changing, and predictability tends to be a novel experience.

Knowing that we easily get stuck in these predictable patterns, when my son, Sam, was a baby, I chose to create one thing he couldn't predict. I diapered him differently from one time to the next. First, I'd lay him down facing one way. Next time facing another way. Then I'd alternate fastening the diaper from the left or right side first.

Choosing to create an unfamiliar pattern helps the brain adapt. You benefit by not feeling challenged when faced with a change or unexpected event.

When I was married to Neal, his close friend told me one day, "If you and Neal won a free trip on the Concorde to Paris, but you must leave in the morning, you'd be on the trip without him."

She knew how happy it made him when he had time to plan and prepare. Unexpected events even pleasurable often send people into chaos.

Where do you get stuck? When I recommend changing the familiar early morning routine to clients I usually hear, "No way. I just can't do it. It'd mess my whole day up."

My comment is, "What is more difficult, changing the routine or being stuck when you're looking at a much bigger change in your life?"

Helping your brain learn to adapt more easily serves you when the bigger stuff looks you in the eye. I suggest changing the simple early morning ritual of starting your day. If you brush your teeth before you shower, do it after you shower. If you put your right shoe on first, start alternating left foot first. Change will prove less of a challenge for you.

Cortex Matures in the Mid-20s

As a child grows, the cortex system grows reaching full maturity around age 25. The cortex system is the higher brain center usually referred to as the "thinking brain." Neurologists sometimes refer to it as the "new" brain. The cortex controls rational thinking, reasoning, logic, organization, impartiality, rules, competition, planning, manipulation, accomplishment and problem solving.

Before I go any further please note that the cortex reaches full maturity in adulthood. This has nothing to do with intelligence. Smart teenagers have mature limbic systems and growing cortex systems. Add hormones and you have the typical teenager making emotionally based decisions.

Until their mid-twenties that is what they are capable of doing. Now do you understand why smart kids make irrational decisions based on their emotions? Give them a few more years, when they reach their mid-20s. They'll make better decisions.

Observe Emotions with the Cortex

The cortex also allows you to observe your emotions. You can think about your emotions as well as describe them.

When you are filled with emotions and expressing them through passive, passive aggressive or aggressive behavior, you are disconnected from the cortex. The cortex, the thinking brain center, enables you to solve problems. When you do not have access to the cortex you give away your power to the emotions.

If you are being rational without acknowledging your feelings you are still suppressing emotion. You don't have access to your wisdom. The most creative response to the situation continues to elude you.

Brain Metaphor

Think about a new computer as a metaphor for the brain. The new computer arrives. You take it out of the box and place it on your desk. Plug it in and Windows 2000 comes up along with the usual computer company installed software. Consider the hardware, operating system and software the limbic system.

Does the computer handle all your business needs? No, of course not. You still have to enter your own data. The data represents the cortex.

Will the computer do the job using just the data without Windows or the programs? No. To handle your tasks and be able to use the data to solve problems you need all the components: hardware, operating system, software and data.

The same dynamic happens with the brain. If you only use the limbic system you don't have the data (your input). If you only use the cortex and not acknowledge your feelings, you don't have the operating system and software (survival needs).

When you use the whole brain, you acknowledge your feelings and the facts of the situation. Then you can come up with the most creative solution to a problem.

Whole Brain Wisdom

Accessing the whole brain allows you to use your wisdom and intuition to formulate the creative solution. You will experience calm, detached, loving, compassion, undemanding, peaceful control. This is when you experience your full power.

Deepok Chopra, M.D. says,
"When a person stops focusing on outer activity, closes his eyes, and relaxes, the brain activity automatically alters. The dominance of alpha wave rhythms signals a state of rest that is aware at the same time. The brain doesn't go to sleep. It isn't thinking either.

"Instead there is a new kind of alertness, one that needs no thoughts to fill up the silence. Corresponding changes occur in the body at the same time, as blood pressure and heart rate decrease, accompanied by lessened oxygen consumption.

"These various changes do not sound overly impressive when put in technical terms, but the effect can be dramatic. Peace replaces the mind's chaotic activity; inner turmoil ceases."

The act of observing your emotions immediately moves you into a whole brain response. That observation enables you to acknowledge your emotions and the facts of the situation. Now the most creative solution is available. Notice you will be breathing deeper too.

Rapid Recall

> ➤ How can you use these concepts and tools in this chapter?

> ➤ What can you do differently?

> ➤ What steps are you willing to take, starting now, to put this into action?

> ➤ What will happen if you do this for 30 days?

> ➤ How will your life change?

Notes

Chapter Five

Power, Keep It or Lose It

"Truth is within ourselves; it takes no rise from outward things, whatever you may believe: There is an inmost center in us all, where truth abides in fullness."
—Robert Browning

Have you touched a doorknob in the winter and gotten a shock? When you walk across a wool carpet on a dry cold winter day the electricity builds.

During a talk at the Ritz Carlton Hotel in Atlanta, every time I wanted to shake hands I'd feel these sparks of electricity. What we are experiencing is excess electricity discharging from our body.

Sometimes we act as if we are a lamp plugged into a light socket so we can get juiced and turn on. This surge of electricity/juice is the emotion from your limbic center (emotional brain) plugging into another limbic center. I call this the *Limbic Dance*. When you move into your emotional drama along with someone else you begin the *Limbic Dance*.

Kinetic Energy

In physics, kinematics is the study of motion exclusive of the influences of mass and force. In layman's terms, the energy (the juice) that passes through a physical body or thing is known as kinetic energy.

This is similar to the kinetic energy that passes through an automobile pileup on the freeway. One car hits another and causes a chain reaction.

In my presentations, I demonstrate how kinetic energy relates to what we think. Kinetic energy will either let us keep our power and strength or physically weaken our body.

First, I ask the group, "Who bench presses?" I'm looking for the perceived strongest person in the room. The volunteer joins me at the front of the room. For this exercise let us call him George.

George stands facing away from the group either looking at a wall or out a window. I don't want him distracted by people. Then I lead him through the following exercise.

1. Standing directly behind George with my left hand on his right shoulder, George extends his right arm to his right at shoulder level. He makes a fist.

2. Placing my right hand on his right arm just above the elbow, I ask him to resist me pushing his arm down. This is to test his level of strength.

3. Now I ask George to resist the pressure from my hand while he says three times out loud, "My name is George, my name is George, my name is George." He will be very strong.

4. Changing the pressure from my right hand I just use my first finger on my right hand. I repeat #3 except George makes up a name. "My name is Hugh, my name is Hugh, my name is Hugh." George will not be able to resist the pressure of just my finger. He will be weaker.

5. Continuing to apply pressure above his right elbow with my right first finger, George resists while he remembers a time when he was passive, aggressive or passive aggressive. He will be weak. This is only a memory. It would be just as weak if he were acting out his emotions in an unhealthy way vs. thinking about it.

6. Then George recalls a time when he started to use inappropriate behavior but instead he chose to handle his emotions and talk about the issue in a responsible way. He was able to resolve the situation and get his needs met. When I apply pressure with my whole hand, George is strong.

6. Now I invite Liz to join us. She becomes the speaker and George continues to have his strength tested.

7. First, the speaker, Liz, touches George's left arm or holds his left hand with her right hand. Liz says her name three times, "My name is Liz...." George, resisting the pressure of my hand, is strong.

8. Next Liz says three times, "My name is George," while I apply pressure with my right first finger. George will be weak.

9. Liz now recalls a time when she used inappropriate behavior and didn't handle her emotions responsibly. George will not be able to resist the pressure of my right first finger.

10. Liz will think about a time she chose to use responsible behavior when she'd been upset and talk it through to a successful conclusion. Using all my strength to push down George's arm with my hand, he will be very strong. It's usually stronger than steps 3-9.

Let's discuss what happened. When George spoke his personal truth, "My name is George," it strengthened him. When he didn't speak his personal truth, "My name is Hugh," he grew weak (Steps 3 and 4).

When Liz spoke her personal truth, "My name is Liz," George was strong. When Liz did not speak her truth, "My name is George," he was weak. Even though it was George's name, Liz was speaking as if it was her name. It wasn't her personal truth (Steps 8 and 9).

Was there any intention to lie? No, they were following instructions. Whenever you are not candid with yourself or any one else you give away your power. Your body becomes physically weaker.

The brain does not know the difference between remembering actions and the actual time of action. When you are *just thinking* about inappropriate behavior you give away your power and you become physically weaker.

The human body is similar to a battery with electricity running through it. It is these electrical responses that allow a lie detector machine to work.

The same principles apply when you are just thinking, remembering or acting out inappropriate and unhealthy behavior: passive, aggressive or passive aggressive. You will lose your physical strength and power.

I have performed this exercise with success, without exception, in groups all over the United States and Canada for the past several years. Even my son learned this when he was only six-years-old.

When you are candid, communicating respectfully along with responsible actions **YOU are powerful.** So is everyone else.

Do you ever come home from the office tired after being in meetings all day? What is physically exhausting about being in meetings? You are tired because you or someone else was not speaking candidly in respectful ways. All it takes is one person in the group to make everyone else weak. Recently a CEO in New York told me his story.

Ken realized he needed to downsize his company to keep it from going under, a very difficult and painful decision. Ken called a meeting with his key people. He told them he had to let go 22% of the staff. He also said it would strengthen the organization for the long term.

Ken solicited their help to choose who would stay. His executive committee rolled up their sleeves and they spent the day reorganizing the company.

The question I asked, "Did you feel energized or tired at the end of the day?"

Surprised, Ken said, "Everyone was energized and it has continued. They're working hard making these difficult changes. There is no negative feedback from my key people."

The difficulty of the situation does not determine your energy level. Rather, your honesty with yourself affects your stamina. Taking control changes everything.

If you are engaged in physical labor like carrying cement blocks, you will need to watch this very carefully to maintain your strength. Pay attention to your thoughts and actions. You may find new levels of strength to perform your tasks.

Rapid Recall

> ➤ How can you use these concepts and tools in this chapter?

> ➤ What can you do differently?

> ➤ What steps are you willing to take, starting now, to put this into action?

> ➤ What will happen if you do this for 30 days?

> ➤ How will your life change?

Notes

Chapter Six

Anger, Rage and Hostility

"If one comes across a person who has been shot by an arrow, one does not spend time wondering about where the arrow came from, or the individual who shot it, or analyzing what type of wood the shaft is made of, or the manner in which the arrowhead was fashioned. Rather, one focuses on immediately pulling out the arrow."

—*Shakyamuni, the Buddha*

Anger, rage and hostility are secondary emotions. We express anger, rage or hostility because we do not have the courage to talk about our *fears*.

When our expectations and needs are not met, we usually get angry because we fear something may happen. After working with 600 plus CEOs on this particular issue, I've learned it isn't easy to acknowledge the fears.

Let me share an example that I encountered in one of my Canadian sessions.

Bob talked about his teenage son being lazy. He spent too much time watching television. He didn't engage in sports. His grades were not acceptable. Bob was angry. This is not an unusual story.

When I asked Bob what scared him, he answered, "My son may not graduate from school."

I asked again, "What are you afraid of?"

He responded, "He won't be successful in life."

I pressed him. "If he isn't successful, what are you afraid will happen?"

"He won't be happy," he said.

I took it one step further. "What happens if he isn't happy?"

Bob took a deep sigh. "I will have failed as his Dad."

I quietly asked, "Do you still feel angry?"

"No," he quickly responded.

When you are willing to look behind the anger and find the fear, the rage and anger instantly disappears, as does the tension that has been resonating in the body as we discussed in chapter two, Body Beware.

Observing Dr. Phil McGraw work with several couples that had been raging for a minimum of 10 years, taught me a great deal about anger. When they allowed themselves to be vulnerable and express their fears and needs, the rage instantly disappeared.

Risks for Heart Disease

Dr. Redford Williams at Duke University and Dr. Robert Sapolsky at Stanford University have conducted studies that demonstrate that anger, rage and hostility are particularly damaging to the cardiovascular system. The evidence has now confirmed what we always thought. Hostility does have harmful effects and is a major risk factor in heart disease. It is believed to be equal to, or perhaps greater than, the traditionally recognized risk factors such as high cholesterol or high blood pressure.

We can express anger, rage and hostility in any one of three ways: passive, aggressive or passive aggressive behavior.

Working with many people on these issues of anger and hostility, I have recognized four basic patterns. If you have done any experience with behavioral diagnostic tools similar to The Interaction Profile produced by Greene Alliances, Inc. you will easily understand these concepts. I encourage you to visit our website http://www.communicatingworks.com to learn more about them.

Fear – Your Achilles Heel

Over the past 14 years I've administered The Interaction Profile to thousands of people in Fortune 100 companies nationwide. Fear appears in four different ways based on the behavior you are acting out at the time.

Fear of Powerlessness – the Need is to Be in Control
Fear of Failure – the Need is to Be Right
Fear of Abandonment – the Need is to Be Included
Fear of Conflict – the Need is for everyone to Be Friendly with each other

Bob fears failure. He needs to raise his son the "right" way for him to be happy and successful. He fears his son may become a failure.

One of my clients, previously a Top Gun pilot, now a senior executive for a large international organization, chose to share this with me.

"This has opened up a whole new world for people to understand how to talk to each other to get their point across without seeming angry, frustrated or inflaming the situation. We now have the tools to understand how we process information differently.

"It filled a gap that we had as a team in communicating effectively without judging our feelings or perception to others. It has helped me understand the needs of my team and how to tailor my message to be the most effective I can be in communicating and motivating."

People can go through a range of fears, one or two more intense than the others. It is your Achilles heel. A non-profit executive and a wonderful, fun mother shared this with me.

"Over the past ten years I have been dealing with many core issues surrounding growth through a divorce and fears of not surviving alone while raising three sons. The fears often overwhelm me. Fear of financial shortages, fear of not having the time to properly care for my children, fear of never having fun again, fear of growing old alone all have been my demons at night.

"Projecting into the future and self-judgment has caused blind spots to reality. Working with these principles has helped me quickly see reality rather than illusion. Then the intensity of the issue dissipates and I see the truth of the situation."

Take a minute and think about something that makes you crazy! Can you look underneath the anger and recognize the fear? What unrealized expectation or need drives the fear? Your unfulfilled needs frighten you, and the fear fuels the anger.

Anger is a Signal

Anger can prove productive in your life. Anger signals you that something is wrong or not at peace within you. The key is to recognize the anger and release it *immediately*.

Remember as long as you hold onto the anger you give away your power. The anger has the power. You lose strength. Take action from a strengthened position not a weak one.

When you express anger by projecting it outward through sarcasm, revenge, bullying, hitting, etc., you lose control and give away your power to the anger.

When you project your anger inward through denial, stuffing your feelings, you feel down in the dumps. If allowed to build, it will grow into depression. Again you lose control and give away your power to the anger.

Abandonment is my Achilles heel. If I feel angry, I am feeling abandoned. I ask myself, "How am I being excluded?" Then I communicate my fears and what I choose in that moment.

False Expectations Appearing Real

Since we are discussing candor and our "personal truth" let us look at F-E-A-R. Rob Brown says, FEAR is **F**alse **E**xpectations **A**ppearing **R**eal. Fear is not real, but what we imagine may happen. I personally believe that if we spend time thinking about a fear every day, it will become a reality. Here is my true story.

My dear friend, Donna had a little girl named Katherine. Dick, the father, insisted Donna not drive on the freeway with

Katherine to see friends or family. He was only comfortable for Donna to drive with her to the local grocery store or other shops close by. He was afraid they'd be in an accident.

On Katherine's sixteenth birthday she received her first car a Jeep Cherokee with big wheels. The very first time driving without her parents she stopped at a red light. Across the intersection a police car came speeding towards her and hit the Jeep head on.

Katherine's friend was thrown out of the Jeep. The engine was pushed inside the Jeep trapping Katherine. Without the big wheels the engine would have killed them. Her foot was caught underneath the gas pedal. Both the police car and the Jeep were totaled. The EMS team cut open the door and the pedal to release Katherine.

Miraculously both girls had minor injuries. Later that evening Donna called me about the tragic accident. I immediately reacted. "Dick has feared Katherine would be in an accident since the day she was born. The first time she drove her own car, sixteen years later, she was in an accident!"

The Facts Don't Matter

Sylvia Crowley of Colorado women's basketball team, says her motto is, "If the dream is big enough, the facts don't matter."

I believe, "If the fear is big enough, the facts don't matter." Sixteen years holding onto a fear is big enough. Are you holding onto a fear? Remember it's not a reality, only your imagination.

You've heard the old adage, "Be careful of what you wish for." Let's reframe that. *"Be careful of what you fear."*

Choose

Notice I said choose vs. need. Does someone who desperately needs money get a loan from the bank? Does a beggar easily attract money? No, they are needy. Neediness repels what it wants to attract.

When you choose, you change the dynamics. Say out loud, "I need a loan." Now say out loud, " I choose to get a loan." Can you feel the difference between those two statements? Use the word; choose as often as you can. Let me know what happens.

Think of a time when you were very angry.

> Can you see the primary emotion?

> Reach behind the anger and discover your true feelings.

> What were these feelings of vulnerability and fears?

> The moment you express these true feelings, the anger gently disappears.

Release Anger, Rage & Hostility

How do you release anger, rage and hostility? Ask yourself, "What is my fear? What expectations aren't being met?" Then ask for what you want. An adapted model of The Anger Ladder from Dr. Ross Campbell's book *How to Really Love Your Teenager* is on the "Brain at Work" video. When I show this segment during my presentations, the usual response is absolute silence. Think of anger as having 15 levels or rungs on a ladder starting with one at the bottom—pleasant behavior to 15 at the top—the most destructive level of anger.

1. Pleasant behavior
2. Seeking resolution
3. Focusing anger on source only
4. Holding onto the primary complaint
5. Thinking logically and constructively
6. Unpleasant and loud behavior
7. Cursing
8. Displacing anger to source other than original
9. Expressing unrelated complaints
10. Throwing objects
11. Destroying property
12. Verbal abuse
13. Emotional destructive behavior
14. Physical abuse
15. Passive aggressive behavior

Psychiatrists tell us **it's more difficult to heal the victims of passive aggressive behavior than victims of physical violence.**

Take a deep breath. Let's discuss this further. Physical violence is direct and open. You know the perpetrator. It is clearer what the issues are and easier to work through. Physical wounds are easier to heal than deep emotional wounds.

Passive aggressive behavior is subtle and insidious. When someone you love sees you hurt after they made a passive aggressive remark they may say:

> - "I was just kidding!"
> - "I didn't mean anything by it."
> - "Can't you take a joke?"
> - "I only said it...I didn't do it."

After awhile, the victim of the passive aggressive behavior starts believing they created the situation. They feel undeserving. Because they love the person who hurts them, they stop trusting their own intuition. Usually it becomes a series of emotional abuse incidents over a longer period of time. Most victims of passive aggressive behavior develop many relationships that exhibit the same traits.

Dr. Brenda Davies said, "If passive aggressive victims do not receive help, they sometimes express all this hostility by acting out with aggression. While everyone else sits around and claims no responsibility, the victim explodes and becomes violent."

In a presentation in California last year, we took a break after viewing the Anger Ladder from the "Brain at Work." Dan called his wife. This is how he related the conversation.

Dan: Kelly, the funny guy you married isn't going to be as funny anymore. I've just learned sarcasm is not really so funny. I'm going to stop the sarcastic comments with our two son-in-laws. (Sigh)

Kelly: (Excited) Oh, Dan that's wonderful.

Dan: (Annoyed) Wonderful! What do you mean? I'm not going to be the funny guy you know!

Kelly: (Compassionate) Dan, it will create much better relationships with both of them. I am so glad. This is not about being funny. It's about having a meaningful relationship.

In the documentary, *Vietnam - The Season for Healing*, the opening caption reads, *"Healing the open wounds of the flesh are easier than pains in the heart."*

Healthy Humor

From discussing this subject with many people throughout North America, I realize the great challenge is finding humor in things other than making fun of the people we know. The funniest humor derives from laughing at us rather than each other.

Clients who come for coaching have shared many similar experiences. Now we have profound processes for healing emotional issues that lack the gut wrenching appeal of the old psychiatric models used in the 80s and 90s. These new processes boast a new gentleness and timeliness in transforming the dynamics within us and in our relationships.

Rapid Recall

➤ How can you use these concepts and tools in this chapter?

➤ What can you do differently?

➤ What steps are you willing to take, starting now, to put this into action?

➤ What will happen if you do this for 30 days?

➤ How will your life change?

Notes

Chapter Seven

The Art of Candor

"We remain in struggle when we are attached to our emotional drama."

—*Susan E. Greene*

When offended, upset or irritated, Anke Nowicki told one of her clients, "Report your feelings." Whether we direct our emotions inward or project them outward to someone else there is a proven, effective way to utilize the brain to better manage the situation. I call it ***"Report. Report. Report."*** and refer to it as the art of candor.

Being Authentic

Our brain remembers in pictures. Visualize a television reporter. My favorite example is one of the most memorable moments in television reporting.

Some of you will recall when Walter Cronkite announced JFK's assassination in 1963. He took off his glasses and wiped a tear from his face. He was being authentic.

He shared genuine emotion then told us the facts. He would equally have been effective if he said, "I am sad to report…."

He wasn't sobbing. That would have been too distracting and manipulative. He broke the golden rule in broadcasting. Don't show your emotion when reporting the news.

Although many years have passed, we still remember that very powerful moment. Cronkite's authenticity captured our full attention. We heard everything he had to say.

Reporting to Yourself

On my way to Galveston where I was giving a keynote address to Fina and BASF Petrochemicals, I was driving my Jeep in the outside lane going 70 MPH. In the lane next to me, one car length ahead, I noticed an 18-wheeler hauling a flatbed traveling at the same speed.

All of a sudden a large iron pipe, approximately 8 feet long and 6 inches wide, came rolling out from underneath the flatbed above the wheels. My first thought was it's going to hit my windshield. I responded by slowly stepping on my brakes. While looking in the rearview mirror at the speeding traffic behind me, I watched the iron pipe move through the air toward me.

Everything suddenly went into slow motion and my mind went into overdrive. The next realization was it was going to hit the front of the Jeep. No…it is falling and will hit and slash the tires. No…I'm going to drive over the pipe…thank God…I have four wheel drive. No…it is rolling off to the side of the road.

Okay, I'm fine. I didn't create a major car pileup on Interstate 45. I accelerated and continued on my trip to Galveston.

Upon reflection, I realized that I responded to the situation rather than reacted to it. I never played the drama queen role that I know so well. Instead, I focused on the facts, didn't panic and allowed the miracle of the pipe to roll out of harm's way.

"Report. Report. Report." gives you a powerful tool to talk to yourself as well as communicating with others. Television newscasters know this. It is the technique they use to report a story. They report the facts of the event as well as their emotions as an observer.

Other people skilled using this tool includes EMS workers, 911 telephone operators, trauma care teams, pilots and astronauts.

Reporting is a Whole Brain / Heart Response

On the television special, *The Brain at Work,* produced by PBS, Dr. Kotrla from Baylor College of Medicine endorsed this technique as an effective way to handle emotions in an appropriate way.

The steps in *REPORT! REPORT! REPORT!*

1. **Observe** you are upset.

2. **Pay attention** to your body's alarm system. Remember we discussed how irritations lead to stress reactions in the body. Pay attention to where the stress and tension resonate in your body.

   This is what the brain does in response to the fight or flight trigger. It is dumping adrenaline and stress hormones throughout your body in response to your thoughts or emotions.

3. **Choose** to handle your emotional reactions.

4. Take a **deep breath**. This will oxygenate the brain and heart.

5. **Report** by **describing your emotions.** Start with your concerns, the needs not being met. Describe them from an observer's point of view, versus project them onto the other person or inward by stuffing your emotions.

6. **Talk about the facts** of the situation. Think of reporting as if you were a television news reporter describing the situation and the facts from an observer's point of view.

7. **Continue monitoring your breathing**. Whenever you get upset notice you only have shallow breaths.

8. **Listen** until they are **finished**. Continue reporting. You'll become calm and gain control.

Example reporting to others

The local news station is reporting that a major storm with hurricane strength winds is heading towards your community. The storm has already left other communities with catastrophic damage in the storm's path.

The reporter reports all the facts. They tell you about how people are getting ready for the storm. They also talk about the different emotions people are experiencing. The reporter usually talks about the FEAR someone has expressed.

Whatever they report it is always in an observer's point of view. They want to be understood. If they become emotionally dramatic on the air, you the listener will be distracted by their emotions. You won't hear the whole story.

*In practicing these tools with clients I've discovered in the very tough conversations, the most powerful candid conversation begins with talking about the fears and needs. Reframe **need** to what you **choose**. Then talk about your emotions and the facts from an observer's point of view.*

Example reporting to you about Road Rage

Limbic approach:

"You shouldn't have pulled in front of me you_____! If I had a big truck, I'd ram it into your car right NOW!"

Reporting approach:

I can see I'm angry. My shoulders are tense and I'm clenching my jaw and hands. Take a deep breath. I know I'm late. Projecting my frustration onto an inconsiderate driver won't get me there any faster. Relax and enjoy the music on the radio. Breathe.

Example reporting to children

Limbic approach:

"You're always late getting ready for school. You haven't put your dirty clothes in the hamper. You left the wet towel on the floor. You left your breakfast dishes on the table. Your room's a mess! Who do you think I am, your full time maid?"

Reporting approach:

I allow myself to get angry every morning. I walk out of the house all tensed up. No wonder I have to go to the chiropractor so often. Breathe. I blame my children for being late when I'm really mad at myself for not getting up earlier and being more organized. I'm going to put a list on the bathroom door to remind them to hang up the towels and use the hamper. Breathe. Instead of yelling and barking orders

I'll ask for their help because I have so much to do in the mornings. I will smile and remember to tell them I love them.

Example reporting in a relationship

Limbic approach:
 "You never listen. I'm overwhelmed with chores and you sit and watch the ballgame all night. When do I get a break? I come home, help the kids with homework, cook dinner, do the dishes, wash a load of clothes, make sure the kids get bathed, pack lunches and finally crawl upstairs to bed without enough energy to spend ten minutes reading a book before falling asleep! We never have time to just relax together!"

Reporting approach:
 "I'm overwhelmed. I feel the stress all over my body."
Breathe.
 "I see you've had time to relax by watching the ballgame. I feel frustrated with so much to do this evening. Please help the kids with their homework. I'm sure during the breaks and halftime will work. Also please help me by putting the wash in the dryer. That will give me time to enjoy a bath and read for 30 minutes before I go to sleep. I'd like to talk for a few minutes after the game and catch up on our day. Thanks, Honey."

 Sometimes even if you are reporting, the other person may get angry and lash back. Remember they react because they have an unrealized expectation. This need creates fear that drives anger.

For example:

My friend, Lynn has been producing an organization's monthly newsletter listing the activities and the members' advertising. She was not pleased because Ken, the manager, hadn't upheld their agreement. Besides not being paid for additional time and work, Lynn no longer enjoyed the work.

Lynn called Ken to give her 30-day notice. Ken's unkind and unprofessional reaction surprised Lynn. Ken was angry and probably disappointed that he had to find someone else to do the work. He had deadlines and was afraid he couldn't find someone in time. The fear drove the anger.

Lynn took this personally and felt very hurt but Ken only acted out of fear.

In a similar situation you can respond by saying, "I realize your concern that you may not meet your deadline."

"Report. Report. Report." This tool allows you to share your feelings in a respectful manner without the distractions of dumping emotions over someone else. It gives you the platform to ask for what you want. You will be heard.

What happens if someone comes into your office and starts yelling? First, remember fear, and unmet expectations or needs drive their anger. Second, ask them questions to help them talk about what they fear.

➤ What are you afraid may happen?
➤ What are you scared about …..?
➤ You sound really upset. Are you worried about something?
➤ I don't think this is the real issue. What concerns you the most?

Use comfortable language and remember your object: to uncover the fear or concern. Once you have exposed their fear, the anger quickly subsides.

There may be times when you continue to report and the other person doesn't stop being limbic. Some people are too attached to their emotional drama.

Limbic Dance

If you stop reporting, you will engage in the *Limbic Dance*. Disconnecting from the cortex, your wisdom and the creative solution will be totally unavailable. Keep reporting. You have a responsibility to yourself to remain in control and keep your power.

In most situations if you will maintain reporting, you will create the space for the other person to gain control. If you lose control, remember the *Limbic Dance* will begin.

Anger Covers Up the Core Issue

In the many, many client conversations I've discovered that anger covers up lots of stuff. When we practice reporting in our sessions it has taken up to five levels going deeper to uncover the real issue.

It reminds me of an artichoke. First you remove the outer leaves, then the next layer until you discover the heart, the core issue. You cannot find peace with the situation until you come face to face with the core issue and talk about it.

Quite often people argue about the anger, not the real issue. That is why it is difficult to resolve what is really bothering them.

Understanding Emotions

> Emotions are real, natural, healthy and necessary

> Emotions are physical reactions to a stimulus

> Emotions are the body's alarm system

> Emotions allow us to feel loved and loving

> Emotions help us be compassionate

> Emotions enable us to show appreciation

> Suppressing emotions is unhealthy

> Expressing emotions in respectful ways is healthy and responsible

Suppress feelings of fear by expressing anger; you suppress all feelings of joy.

Practice Builds a New Brain Synapse Connection

As with any new learning it takes practice. Just like learning to ride a bike, you think you know how until you get on the first time. Then you practice, practice, practice. Before you realize it you can ride a bike with no hands. Ten years later you jump on a bike and you ride it without even thinking about it.

Practice reporting until one day it comes as easy as riding a bike.

An east coast client sent me this story:

"We're a professional staffing organization. It's been a rough 9 months, due to the total turnover of our sales and recruiting force during October and November. The financial status wasn't that great; a fact I'd shared with a salesperson before he joined.

"Our bank helped us through a temporary cash crunch. The new salesperson was concerned and asked what was going on. After sharing all the details with him, I received this email:

"I really appreciate you taking time to discuss things with me yesterday. That conversation is an example of why I am very happy with my decision to join this company. Knowing we can be open and work through things is going to be the key to our success. You have my utmost dedication. I am sure there will be bumps. No doubt we will look back in a year and be proud of what we built. I appreciate your support. Thanks for the opportunity.

"Another experienced recruiter responded to our ad. During the interview, I shared with her our financial situation. She thanked me. Then said that only made her want to join us even more. The challenge and honesty were a real draw for her.

"All our support staff knew our financial situation though none have left. Instead, they've contributed, above and beyond, ideas that pushed us into several new promising areas.

"All of which speaks volumes about trust and the power of candor."

Do you have the luxury of time to wait for any discussion? Reporting allows you to tell the truth with grace and compassion. Reporting creates the necessary safety to talk about challenging situations at the moment they occur. You feel heard. Trust will grow. A friend shared this difficult conversation with me last year:

"Had a humiliating and possible debilitating experience with the staff this week – but your reporting technique saved me. I was having lunch with the executive, assistant executive and staff administrator after a Board meeting. I was relaying the actor's point of view on the difficulty of stopping production to get the paper work done.

"The assistant executive exploded with anger, banging his fists on the table and began yelling, 'Why the hell am I wasting my time if my own damn president doesn't even know how to stand up to the producers...

"After a couple sentences of his harangue, I suggested he calm down so we could discuss this. He refused and continued yelling about his disgust. I briefly went into the defensive mode and made a feeble suggestion that perhaps I am not the right person for the presidency. The exec stepped in to say that I was, 'for the time being.'

"I thought of you and took a breath. Then I refocused the discussion to the problem of actor empowerment and the assistant exec left the restaurant to cool down. We returned to the office with enough tension to choke a horse!

"I talked to the assistant exec alone. I expressed my dismay at his outburst and made it clear that it was not the message that I objected to, but his method. I told him that I felt humiliated and his action was inappropriate.

"I pointed out that had I dissolved into my emotions (left

and resigned immediately), the results could have been catastrophic to the organization. I listened to his frustrations and accepted his apology when offered. Then as more constructive conversations continued, the exec joined us.

"The assistant exec offered his apology again. The apology offered in front of the exec presented the opportunity for rebuilding trust. There was a feeling we had all achieved a new level of understanding and respect for each other."

Problems Caring for Aging Parents

With science making so much headway in medicine, people are living longer. Many of you can enjoy having your parents and grandparents active in your lives until their later years. I loved being with my Mother's parents who lived well into their 90's.

Today we are creating stories about the new millennium that we'll share with our grandchildren. I was lucky to have a grandfather who was 94 when he died in 1967.

He told fascinating stories about growing up in Ireland, immigrating with my great grandparents and passing through Ellis Island before the turn of the century. I loved hearing him talk about paving the dirt roads in New York City as a construction engineer, and his other experiences. My favorite story was about Grandfather owning one of the first cars built in America. He liked playing practical jokes.

Grandfather rigged a second tank next to the gas tank. He'd seriously ask the gas attendant to fill the tank up with water, not gas. Then he'd put two mothballs into the water tank, get back in the car and drive off leaving the people in the gas station very surprised as well as his friends in the car.

As a young girl, I loved hearing the romantic story about

how he met a young woman and finally married when he was 50. My grandmother was 21 and she reported he was the "catch of the county."

My mother would often say to me, "Your grandfather isn't really like that."

I'd respond, "Mom, you may not have been close with grandfather but that's your relationship. We have our own relationship that has nothing to do with yours."

The gifts he gave me were his love, time and teaching me the joy of playing scrabble which is still with me today.

Grandmother became a very independent widow who loved to travel. On the spur of the moment she'd head to North Carolina for a week, driving alone for hours. Towards the end of her life, she'd have unexpected blackouts making it necessary for her to give up driving.

Her caretaker could drive her wherever she wanted to go, but as long as Grandmother had her own keys she insisted on driving. We had to sell the car. As soon as I flew home, she went to the car dealership and bought another.

This was not working. Wishing my mother was still here; I flew back and had a very difficult conversation with my grandmother whom I loved dearly.

"Grandmother, I know you enjoy being independent. It's fun to get up and go as you please. You have someone here to take you in her car whenever and wherever you'd like to go. Now that you're having these blackouts without any notice, it's dangerous to drive. If you have a blackout while driving you may be killed.

"You've traveled extensively. You've had a full, rich life filled with wonderful memories. I want you to really think about the possibility of you having an accident. Don't think only of yourself. You may kill a young mother and her children in the other car.

"We aren't taking away your freedom. You have many available options for getting around. Hannah is always available or you can call a taxi or a friend. I'm asking you to think about the serious consequences if you drive again."

Lou told me he was angry that his mother had stopped visiting his dad everyday in the nursing home. Lou felt she had abandoned his father. Here's his story:

"I flew to see my mother recently and had a candid conversation about my concerns for my father. I told her of my guilty feelings living so far away to visit often.

"I learned my mother's less frequent visits were being caused by her declining physical condition as well as her concerns about 'being a bother' to neighbors who give her rides. She's afraid to spend money for taxi fare. There was a time in our lives when we were very poor. She never handled the money and there is more than enough if they both live to 100 years old.

I realized that at 80 years old, I couldn't expect her to have the physical strength and mental stamina she once had. She's always been there to do whatever was needed for our family— everything from very menial labor jobs to caring for my father in every possible way as he has had a series of different medical problems over the last 20 years. She has always put herself second.

"She is no longer able to handle the strain of going to the nursing home daily and pushing my father's wheel chair for five hours. My mother now needs support and attention too. Clearly she's going through many changes.

"She lives alone, 1200 miles from her only family member she can confide in. Wishing she could be more active and do

more was a struggle. She also knows her husband will be gone soon.

"I've clearly not given her situation enough consideration. Instead I was focused on my father who has more serious medical problems. Now that I recognize her needs better I can be more help to my mother.

"I no longer have the unanswered questions about why she appeared to be abandoning my father that made me angry. Learning how to be candid with my mother and me has benefited both of our lives. Thank you."

Have you been brutally honest with you? Do you have any troubling thoughts or concerns you've not expressed directly with someone else?

As you can see from these personal stories, it keeps you in struggle until you have the conversation. Reporting allows you to deal with any tough situation the moment it happens. Once you experience using this tool effectively, you won't wait to have another difficult conversation again.

Candor Exercise

Now that you have the why and the how, it is time to practice the art of candor through **Report! Report! Report!**

The most important conversation in any relationship is the one you're not having. You both know what it is. What would happen if you had the conversation now?

Using the skills, it is time to practice. The result will be more trust and deeper relationships. More importantly, you will know it is safe to talk about tough issues especially when you feel vulnerable.

Client groups, couples and individuals have shared that they receive more support within their relationships than they had experienced before. Let's practice.

- Recall a recent angry conversation or a time when you were too angry to have the conversation.

- Describe your emotions.

- Where does the tension and stress resonate in your body?

- Notice your breathing. Is it shallow or deep breaths?

- What are the emotions starting with the concerns and the needs that haven't been met? Write them down as if you were reporting them to the other person.

- What are the facts? Write them down.

- What do feel the other person would do if you had reported instead of reacting with anger?

Rapid Recall

- ➤ How can you use these concepts and tools in this chapter?

- ➤ What can you do differently?

- ➤ What steps are you willing to take, starting now, to put this into action?

- ➤ What will happen if you do this for 30 days?

- ➤ How will your life change?

Notes

Chapter Eight

Stop the Story

"Almost always it is the fear of being ourselves that brings us to the mirror."

—*Antonio Porchia*

Triggers can unconsciously set off a series of emotions that plunge you into struggle. Clients say it feels like being a gerbil on a wheel, being on a merry-go-round, in a prison or on a short circuit. Do you live on an emotional roller coaster? Regardless what you call it, it runs you and you lose control.

Get Out of Struggle

To get out of struggle you can pay attention to the triggers and choose in the moment to not run the story. I used to have the story about my divorce. I told it over and over again especially when I was scared there wasn't enough money to take care of Sam and me.

The stories I often hear are about blaming our childhood for choosing poor relationships, blaming our boss for being unhappy at work, feeling guilty for not having enough time with our children, ashamed of being married more than once....

Stop the story. Report by describing your emotions and explain the facts from an observer's point of view. No excuses, no blame, no guilt, no shame, no justification, no regrets, no judgments and no projections. Immediately the struggle stops.

Friday morning at 10:00 AM, sitting on my couch and gazing out my patio door. The patio looked lovely and the sun shone through the large tree creating a dappled light on all the plants. I loved the peace of the moment with *Beethoven's Fifth Symphony* playing in the background.

From nowhere, the "critical committee" entered. You know the voices inside your head, all filled with a variety of judgments. You may call it self-talk or mind chatter. Regardless it is filled with judgments.

This particular morning, two appeared, *Sarcastic (S) and Defensive (D)*:

(S): Why are you sitting on the couch at 10:00 AM and not at the office?

(D): Because I'm going to create a new program for my clients.

(S): Well...you could do it at the office and answer the phone when clients call!

(D): Too many distractions at the office, I prefer the quiet here.

(S): You travel a lot and clients always have to leave a message. You could answer the phone in person for a change!

(D): I only have five hours to prepare this new program. I don't have time.

"Stop! Stop! Stop! I screamed silently to the internal voices. I am not creating the program. I am not at the office answering the phone. I am having a totally ridiculous conversation in my head that adds no value to my life.

Have you ever been there? In that sudden realization I recognized how I justify my actions, my thoughts and what I say. For the next few weeks I observed that I justified everything!!! It was nauseating!

Addictive Thinking Patterns

It is appropriate to justify the principles I share with you in this book. It is appropriate in my presentations. Justification adds very little value in other areas of my life.

The constant need to justify is an addictive thinking pattern. Like any other addiction it needs to be fed. To stop the addiction your only option is to just stop. An alcoholic has to stop drinking. You have to stop justifying everything.

To end this addictive thinking in the beginning I had to say "Stop" at least 20 times a minute. It also meant I couldn't justify why I wanted to stop.

Stopping allowed my mind to go blank. Since nature doesn't like a vacuum, the blank space filled up with a restful silence.

Simple? Very simple. Easy? No way. It takes impeccable diligence. I thought I had it handled. Wrong. Remember this is an addiction. The story continues…

I went to Santa Fe with a friend. He got a cold. And I

started babbling. "You probably got chilled last night getting out of the hot tub on the deck. Look, it's snowing now. It was really cold. Or it might be something you ate that you're allergic to."

This constant addiction to justify everything is awful. I can see my story around judgment showing up too. The awareness hits me in the gut. It makes me feel queasy and lightheaded.

I stopped!

Then all of a sudden I realized my mind was quiet for long periods of time. I discovered that I observed my surroundings with more appreciation.

After six months battling with my critical committee of justification and judgment, I won the war. At every presentation at least one person says, "You are peaceful. I want some of that."

What are your addictive thinking patterns?

Struggle on the Short Circuit Exercise

➢ When you are introduced to a **new concept** or have a **direct experience** how do you respond?

➢ What is your **reaction or feelings** about this concept or experience?

➢ What unconscious reactions do you experience: **excuses, blame, guilt, projection, shame, worry, regret, judgment** or **justification**. I call this the **short circuit**. This is how we **tell our story.**

➢ You can remain in struggle or **choose to consciously move** out of struggle. It is a choice.

➢ Pay attention and choose consciously to stop the addictive thinking patterns. Stop the excuses, blame, guilt, judgment, shame, worry, guilt and justification. **Stop the story.**

➢ Look behind and underneath the frustration and anger. Think about your true feelings and fears. Talk about them to the other person by **Report! Report! Report!**

➢ This process activates the whole brain, cortex and limbic centers with the heart. **Now the most creative solution is available to you.**

This is the art of candor. The result is you honor you. You move out of struggle. You now access your wisdom.

The Promised Secret

What has impacted my life significantly since I stopped these addictive thinking patterns was I discovered *time*. I believe I have another two hours a day. The constant chatter has stopped. Now able to focus without any distractions, I listen without an inner dialogue keeping me from hearing all of what the other person is saying.

More importantly, I hear my inner wisdom. I hear God, spirit, however you refer to that deep guidance that we can completely trust. Answers to questions come quickly. Big decisions are not difficult any more. My work has become very creative and I am learning to really play.

The crowning moment for me came while dealing with two big problems. My son Sam made an interesting comment when we got into the car one day.

He smiled at me and said, "Mom, you are *so* happy."

When I saw the doctor about hormone replacement therapy. He commented, "You live a low stressed life."

Immediately reported, "No, I live a very high stressed life. I've traveled 60,000 air miles in 8 months. I'm a business owner and a single parent...I choose to live with low stress."

Blessed is how I describe my life. When clients trust me and share their pain or where they get stuck, I feel truly honored. Receiving emails and phone calls about their breakthroughs my eyes sweat too.

Many have shared their stories with you. Douglas's story is amazing. I've known Douglas since we were in our teens though we hadn't seen each other for many years.

Enjoying a weekend with Douglas and his grown family, we spent hours talking about the past twenty years and our perspective on life's journey.

Very troubled about work, Douglas had stuffed his anger for a long time. I shared all the concepts and information from this book. He realized he had lived his life in judgment. He'd judged everybody. Judging himself was the most painful.

Douglas stopped the story immediately. I thought it was impossible to do it so quickly. Thank you, Douglas, for having the trust and courage to examine your pain. You took responsibility and didn't blame it on anyone or anything else. Thank you for giving me permission to share your story openly in this book.

"I've spent virtually everyday since our talk pondering on what has happened. For all my life I've been asking myself 'Who am I?' Now, thanks to you, I discovered the answer. For the life of me, I'm unable to tell you or anyone else who I am. Or why I'm here.

"I know that I've had my eyes opened. A veil has dropped and I can see. But what do I see? I can't find the words to describe my vision.

"This machine's vocabulary is simply inadequate. I do know we are invaluable, invincible, untouchable beings. We come from the same source. We are brothers and sisters indeed.

"I believe we are one. We merely occupy different machines that we use in different ways to get around on planet earth.

"Our friendship, our trust, our ability to be honest as well as open with each other helped me see, understand and know. With this knowledge comes power. I now have the strength and courage to just be. to do, to act.

"Don't ask me what I'd do in certain situations. Frankly,

I don't have a clue. I just know there is a source to turn to, an inward source that will provide the answer. It is truly seek and you shall find. Ask and it shall be given. It took me 48 bloody years to discover that!!! Better late than never.

"The second question I've been asking all my life is, 'What am I doing here?' I'm sticking my neck out here…we are here to be love. Pure and simple. Love and be loved. Show it. Express it. Be it in every possible way.

"There is nothing to be afraid of. But that can only be understood and appreciated when you truly know who you are. I paraded through the past 40 years with an artificial plate of armor around me. I thought I was capable of withstanding a nuclear blast from three feet away.

"Despite this, I could be hurt by the slightest barb or odd remark. Now that I feel totally exposed in my new found freedom, totally naked to the world I feel invincible. Deep down inside me I am untouchable. I cannot be affected where it matters by no one!!!

"I am open, more honest, more at ease with my fellow human beings than I have ever been. What has changed? Knowing who I am. We are all alike, there in that core of our being. I am just lucky enough to have discovered the secret and it is there for all to see. Good luck to you. May you open the eyes of the rest of the world. The sooner the better."

Douglas.

Stop the Story!

Rapid Recall

> ➢ How can you use these concepts and tools in this chapter?

> ➢ What can you do differently?

> ➢ What steps are you willing to take, starting now, to put this into action?

> ➢ What will happen if you do this for 30 days?

> ➢ How will your life change?

Notes

Chapter Nine

Life is a Series of Choices

You create your life by your decisions and solutions. Do you choose carefully?

— Susan E. Greene

On my 28th birthday, I buried my mother who was only 49. In October 1999 I celebrated my 50th birthday, healthy and free from heart disease. It was a major milestone. I can't imagine any life being over this young. I am happier than I've ever been.

What if my time was up and that iron pipe came hurdling through my window while I was driving to Galveston.

I can only imagine what my wonderful, loving, 10-year-old son, Sam would say at my funeral.

"I had the 'bestest' Mom. She was fun and happy. She used to be a Drama Mama then she stopped. She would listen and help me when I was mad. She taught me how to observe my third grade teacher throwing passive aggressive comments to us kids and not feel hurt anymore.

"I remember when I was obsessed with the Power Rangers. She showed me how I gave up my power and I couldn't hold my arm up when I said, 'I'm so stupid.'

Mom helped me learn to experience new things and go

discover new places. She always let me have my friends come for sleepovers.

When we discovered the dirt ramps, I was embarrassed because I was too scared to ride my bike down. Mom took me early in the morning to practice before anybody else got there.

"Sometimes we wouldn't go to Marble Slab but create the Sam Slab. My favorite was ice cream with crushed Oreos or Reese's pieces. My friends loved Mom. In second grade my best friend, Chance, gave Mom a Valentine's Day card too.

"When we lived in Round Top, Mom taught me how to find 'peace.' When everything would get crazy back in Houston, she'd remind me it was time to go find my 'peace' again.

"I'm Mom's only son. Dad has three sons. She waited a long time for me. I'm really going to miss my Mom because she told me she loved me no matter what I did. She loved me just for being me."

Have you found peace? Have you had that difficult conversation that keeps robbing your energy? Have you told the people that are important in your life that you love them for just being and they don't have to do anything for it?

Life is about choices. You can choose to stay in the status quo or start digging inside and discover a new way to show up every day.

A beautiful young mother came for coaching when her life was in chaos. When I asked her to share a story, we had lots to pick from. This is the one she chose. I believe it sums up why these tools are valuable and they do make a difference. These are her words:

This has been very interesting, scary, yet the most

rewarding work I've ever done. What made the most difference in my life is the relationship I now have with my son. I still work everyday not to repeat patterns I was taught, however, I am now able to recognize when the old way of doing things comes up.

This process has taught me a healthier, happier and much more peaceful way to deal with my children. Before anger would always be in control. I remember one day my then 18-month-old son was pushing every button.

I totally lost control and yelled at him. Not just a small yell, but also one that scared him. I saw that scary look in his eyes. It immediately reminded me of a scared little girl I knew and how it made her feel when her mother would yell like that at her. That girl was me.

I stopped and grabbed him. I hugged him as hard as I could. We were both crying and I explained to him it was not his fault. I was angry. It was my story that caused me to be angry. I was having a bad moment. It had nothing to do with him. I apologized a million times.

I told him I loved him. After explaining that I didn't like his behavior he calmed down and so did I. I held and rocked him. It became very peaceful. He looked up at me and smiled. Then went off to play. Everything was okay.

I learned to stop myself when an angry feeling arises by counting 5 to 10 and report my feelings rather than yell or scream. The results are much more harmony and peaceful relationships with not only my son but also my family. Best of all I feel better. I have peace. Thanks, Susan. Thank you, God.

Rapid Recall

➤ How can you use these concepts and tools in this chapter?

➤ What can you do differently?

➤ What steps are you willing to take, starting now, to put this into action?

➤ What will happen if you do this for 30 days?

➤ How will your life change?

Notes

Chapter Ten

When Terror Hits Home

"How does life get any better than this?"

—*Gary Douglas*

As I went about my morning routine that eventful September 11, 2001 morning, a voice deep inside of me told me to turn on the television. I muttered something to myself about not needing a weather report and that it's either hot or going to rain. Either way, it wasn't going to effect my day. Yet the internal voice persisted go turn on the television.

I turned it on in time to see the second airplane hit the Twin Towers. I instantly realized, I had just lived through 25 years of peace. It had been years since my daily thoughts had been filled with issues about security opening the mail or concerned that next time I may not be so lucky.

Flashback...London 1974

As I drove home after midnight from a party and entered Smith Square, a bomb blew up the front of Peter Jones department store on the other side of the square. Quickly turning left and heading away from the debris, I didn't see a soul. I literally missed being a casualty by 60 seconds.

For over a year, we experienced regular bomb scares at the hotel where I worked. Elizabeth working behind the security area at Heathrow Airport needed a daily pep talk because she hated being physically searched everyday.

Keris moved from Liverpool to London to join our sales team. While walking down the street with two suitcases, the police stopped and searched her bags. They were suspicious that she was carrying a bomb.

It became our way of life. There would be a bomb scare that sometimes turned out to be real. Then we'd wait to see who claimed responsibility. It was either the IRA (Irish angry for British intervention in the Protestant/Catholic conflict) or the PLO (Middle East/Israel conflict.)

How did we respond in Great Britain during these chaotic times while life in America continued with ease?

We Became Aware

It was interesting knowing no one would steal your purse. Any box, suitcase, shopping bag, briefcase or purse that was unattended was considered a suspicious bomb. We developed an acute awareness and began noticing anything that was unattended. If you discovered something on its own, you didn't want to stay in the area. After awhile this ability to pay attention to your surroundings became effortless. Just like riding a bicycle, it becomes easy with practice.

At the Summer Olympics in Atlanta, no one was paying attention

While consulting with the Coca-Cola Company prior to the Summer Olympics, I chose not to travel to Atlanta during the events. Not because the city was packed with tourists visiting the Olympics, but because the United States did not seem to be fully prepared to avoid a terrorist attack at that time. I believed that the Summer Olympic Games was a prime target for terrorism.

The premonition came true. When the news flashed that a cardboard box containing the bomb was in front of the stage all evening, I said, "The U.S. doesn't have a clue! Twenty years ago in England that box would never have been left unattended or unnoticed for ten minutes let alone all evening."

How do you become more aware?

First you begin to focus on the present. I like to refer to it as being in the moment. Not the past, that's gone. Not the future, it isn't here yet. Being in the moment allows you to be focused and totally present. You can make quick decisions and respond immediately to any situation.

For example, when the pipe came off the truck flying toward me, I quickly responded by slowing down without slamming on my brakes and creating a car pile up on the freeway. If I'd been focused on the future worrying about what *may* happen, I would have been distracted and panicked.

Back in the 1980s going to dinner with my husband we

were stopped by two men at gunpoint in Houston's Sausolita Bar and Grill's parking lot. Later known as Shot Gun Bar and Grill.

Being a Harris County Detective, Neal, carried a badge, though lucky for the men that night he didn't have a gun with him. One man with wild, crazy eyes as if he were on drugs started shooting around our feet.

Neal said, "You don't want to do this. I'm a police officer."

The second man fled. My inner voice told me to run. I ran into the restaurant and called the police. If I had not stayed focused on the moment and listened to that constant inner guidance I suspect I may have been too afraid to run at the right time to get help.

Fear

Let's revisit fear. Gary Douglas, founder of Access, talks about fear from a different perspective. He suggests people handle crisis either by panicking or become very calm and take action. Later they may have an emotional response or get very tired after the immediate crisis.

How do you deal with crisis? Gary says, "If you aren't paralyzed, remain calm and take action, then you do not experience *fear*. You are able to respond in the present."

When you experience fear you are not present. You are projecting into the future.

God, is my Time Up Now?

On a flight to Canada the pilot asked us to put on our seat belts. We couldn't avoid turbulence up ahead.

When I finished eating lunch, the attendant took the tray. I had capped my bottled water and tucked it into the seat pocket when the airplane dramatically dropped in the sky.

Pandemonium broke loose. The man across the aisle didn't have on his seat belt and hit his head on the baggage overhead compartment. Next to him, his young 10-year-old son drenched in Coca-Cola yelled, "Dad, the pilot told us to put on our seat belts!!!"

Every unsecured item flew about the cabin: food, drinks, bags and bodies. The beverage cart tipped over on a passenger.

The elderly woman from India probably in her 80s held onto my arm so hard she left bruises. She was one of many praying out loud. Others were screaming. Some were sobbing.

It was very interesting to me the way I behaved among all this chaos and the unknown. I silently asked God, "Is this it? Is this life over? Sam's too young for me to leave now!"

That deeper inner guidance that I trust implicitly responded, *No you're fine. There'll be 30 minutes of violent turbulence and then it'll stop. You'll arrive safely.*

So I sat there allowing my seat companion to hold my arm as tight as she needed to while I thought with much gratitude I was *not* upgraded today. First Class was a total mess. China, glasses and food were everywhere and on everybody.

What that means to me is I don't experience fear. As I reflect over my 52 years, in every crisis, I was able to remain calm and take action in the moment. Do you experience fear? Are you able to remain in the moment and take action?

Terrorism hits home

Whether terrorism hits New York or your hometown, we can learn how to adapt to the present climate by becoming more aware. Learn how to be in the moment. Here are two exercises you can play with to teach your mind to stay present.

Exercise

➤ Take your shoes off.

➤ Stand on wood or tile floor in socks or stockings.
➤ Being careful, walk as quickly as you can across the room.

➤ What were you thinking as you walked?

➤ Did you find that you were totally focused on the task?

➤ Were you present?

The same thing happens when you walk on snow, ice or mud. Walk down a slanted wet sidewalk without watching what you're doing. This keeps your mind totally in the moment.

Another simple and easy exercise is to focus on breathing. This exercise is quite different than your normal breathing.

➤ What is your favorite color? *Please choose a color other than brown, black or red for this exercise.*

➤ Inhale by pulling the color down through the top of your head into your heart and *fill your lungs* until your abdomen expands.

➤ Push the color back up and exhale out through your mouth. This will naturally tighten your abdomen more.

➤ Again. Inhale by pulling the color down through the top of your head into your heart and fill your lungs until your abdomen expands. Push the color back up and exhale out through your mouth. This will naturally tighten your abdomen more.

➤ One more time... Inhale by pulling the color down through the top of your head into your heart and fill your lungs until your abdomen expands. Push the color back up and exhale out through your mouth. This will naturally tighten your abdomen more.

➤ Write down what happened? What sensations did you experience?

➤ When you are this focused on your breath. Did you become fully present?

➤ Was your mind quiet or noisy?

➤ Can you imagine your day if your mind was quiet for one hour?

➤ What would happen if it lasted all day? This exercise is great for stress relief? Do it often. When you are having difficulty sleeping, this breathing technique may be very helpful. Do it daily. See what happens.

Eckhart Tolle, author of *The Power of Now*, says your mind is a tool to be used for a specific task, and when the task is completed, you lay it down. Usually most people's thinking is repetitive and useless and often negative. "This kind of compulsive thinking is actually an addiction. What characterizes an addiction? Quite simply this: you no longer feel that you have the choice to stop. It seems stronger than you. It also gives you a false sense of pleasure that invariably turns to pain."

If you find yourself in the middle of a difficult situation, keep reporting to yourself. Once you move into fear and your emotions start running you, you're much more easily manipulated. And you can't hear your inner voice that brings guidance when you most need it.

We all breathe and share the same air

For many, these events have caused much heartache and suffering. I see men who have always been the protectors totally stymied by terrorism here in America. They now know they can't protect their loved ones in all situations. Many have lost sleep while they figure out what to do in the event of an attack.

Jim regularly flies on Southwest Airlines to Louisiana. He spent hours thinking about how he'd intervene if the plane were hijacked. I heard the same story from many different men.

Countries throughout the world have been in conflict, war and terrorism, while I've been enjoying 25 years of peace. However, the events of 9-11 have made Americans more aware of what's really happening around the world. We can no longer live in ignorance or indifference. *We all breathe and share the same air*. Our water all comes to earth from the same sky.

When will life get back to normal?

Can we live in the illusion that what happens in one part of the world does not effect us? Have you noticed that our conversations are becoming less prejudicial in 2002? We stopped being so concerned about our ethnicity or how we worship God.

When I walk along the bayou everyone acknowledges each other as they pass by. Elevators are now places of friendly conversation not silence. "USA Today" reported on 10/08/01 that career has dropped from #1 priority to #11.

So what is normal? Anthrax? We used to fear polio. During the outbreaks of AIDS we speculated that we would stop shaking hands to keep from getting AIDS.

After 9-11 we began a new way of life? Americans have opened up their hearts, their minds and their attitudes. We are learning to live in allowance of each other with much more understanding. This is the new, normal way of life.

Peace begins with me

Peace begins with me. Until I acknowledged my anger and no longer use it in my home or at work to manipulate others…I did not know peace. I choose to be responsible for my part of this big puzzle…world peace. I choose to model it to my son. Only then can I know peace. Do you?

Become a part of the solution

What would happen if each person took responsibility for their emotions and stopped projecting them onto others? Do you wonder what it would be like if each of us was accountable for our life and stopped blaming and judging to justify our actions?

You can read about the secluded, gifted children in a Bulgarian monastery at http://jamestwyman.com. They each share a burning question for the adults everywhere. What action would you take if *love* was present now?

Have you ever considered the infinite possibilities when we choose to live peacefully in our homes, at work and in our communities?

Rapid Recall

➢ How can you use these concepts and tools in this chapter?

➢ What can you do differently?

➢ What steps are you willing to take, starting now, to put this into action?

➢ What will happen if you do this for 30 days?

➢ How will your life change?

Notes

Chapter Eleven

All of Life Comes To Us with
Ease and Joy and Glory

"Wherever you put most of your attention is what you value most in your life. And God will give you more of that."
—Gary Douglas

In January 2001, while the first edition of this book was at the printers, I met Gary Douglas, the founder of Access who became a coach and friend. I'm truly greatfull (my preferred spelling). He has helped me move from needing to have the answer to living life in the question.

When something happens, I ask, "how does it get any better than this?" I'm not looking for the answer, I'm asking for the answer to just show up. For example: Jim and I were flying Southwest Airlines when we checked in he received a boarding pass for the A group while I received one for the C group. So I said, 'how does it get any better than this?" Then headed to a seat in the front of C group line and read a book. We weren't near each other. When it came time to board, the agent looked at Jim and asked, "are you traveling alone?" Isn't that interesting? Has a boarding agent ever asked you that? Jim said no and the agent quickly allowed me to board with him.

Moving into our new townhouse, we moved an antique day bed upstairs. Not an easy task. After two men struggled getting it upstairs we discovered it wouldn't go through the doorway. I declared, "how does it get any better than this?"

We couldn't figure out how to dismantle it. The new living room furniture had just arrived so there was no place downstairs for it. What a dilemma! After ten minutes the men decided to take it back downstairs. They hoisted it up over the balcony railing from outside and through the glass sliding doors. How does it get any better than that?

Making plans for our honeymoon in Ruidoso I kept asking the question. After making reservations for a room at Shadow Mountain Lodge that fit our budget I kept asking how does it get any better than that?

Ten days before we left my intuition told me call the owner now. I did and he answered the phone. I asked if their honeymoon cabin, Spurs and Lace had been reserved during the week we were scheduled to be there. Knowing full well it hadn't. What rate would you give us since we're coming for a week? Guess what? He lowered the price $50 per night and it was in our budget. How does it get any better than that?

Monday morning feeling really good on my way to my favorite Pilates exercise class, a truck sped across the intersection and slammed into my Jeep. The engine burst into flames though I didn't see it. I hadn't even realized the air bag had been deployed. People were yelling, get out of the car. Someone arrived with a fire extinguisher and put out the fire before the fire department even got there.

Somebody called an ambulance. Someone brought ice and rubbed my back until it arrived. Witnesses reported to the police that the other driver ran a red light. Jim was out of town and a friend came to get me. He arranged for my totaled Jeep to be towed. Another friend took me to the doctor.

I am alive! It seems angels were surrounding me and all was arranged so easily. How does it get any better than that?

Over the past few years as I discover more peace within I've begun to welcome all of life, not just the good. I know the solutions will be available when I need them. Sometimes they don't arrive until the nick of time. It's the trust that it'll show up when its necessary that creates the security I feel inside.

When the September 11th event occurred, I was able to stay out of drama and trauma. I did not jump into resistance and reaction, instead focused on being quiet, loving and listening, and in the process, discovered compassion for everyone.

During this time, the things that weren't working in my life became clearer. As I allowed them to go new things showed up that are more fulfilling. Since then the business is expanding in a truly fulfilling way. The work is now balanced between corporate consulting and coaching executives and personal growth with coaching couples, individuals and rape victims. Being an International Facilitator for Access, I facilitate classes, workshops and a weekly group.

Most interesting is using all these tools I developed a loving relationship with me. Learning forgiveness and allowance for who I am and what I've created in my past. I'm not the critical judge I used to be of me. Do you judge you? Whew! That seems to get us all twisted up!

In this space, Jim and I have begun the beautiful journey together as partners allowing each other to be all we can be. Wow…the freedom and joy that comes with all that.

To share these evolving years with you I've put it in prose entitled, *"That's an Interesting Point of View."*

That's an Interesting Point of View

Before…
Valued the ability to finance the business,
Establish credit,
Have a Platinum American Express Card.
Checked in at the President's Club.
Flew first class.
All bills paid first.
What am I proving?

Now…
Pay me 10% first,
Bills paid next.
Living on a cash basis,
Created prosperity.
I wonder what it'd be like to honor me first?

Before…
Clients resisted new ideas,
They loved to challenge.
Teamwork meant agreement.
Resistance followed and
Effort was rewarded.

Now...Clients welcome new ideas,
They look for ways to embrace them personally.
Teamwork is allowing different points of view.
Being able to speak the truth creates power.
People begin to choose allowance.
Rewards come easily when
Using their natural abilities and talents.

Before...
Sam and his Dad pushed my buttons.
Frustrated or angry, Sam would get punished.

Now...
Sam learns there are consequences,
Makes new choices.
Mom is in total allowance.

Before...
Thought I didn't judge,
My friends are white, black and
Every color in between.
They are Christian, Jewish,
Unitarian, Catholic and Buddhist.

Now...
Knowing I sometimes still judge me
By the thoughts about my body.
When looking in a mirror.
What is right about this I'm not getting?

Before…
Eating was for pleasure
And soothing emotions.
Sometimes I had sudden
Aches or pain in the body
For no obvious reason.

Now…
The body chooses the food it needs.
It chooses smaller portions and fewer meals.
Sometimes it chooses just meat
Other times it may be grapes.
When sudden pain shows up, ask
Where did this come from?
It goes away.
What does my body know, I
Pretend not to know?

Before…
Another car hit my car,
Less work from all the
Time in physical therapy.
Now…
Time to regroup and
Change my life.
How can I facilitate more joy?

Before…
There were the good guys,
The bad guys and
The men in black.
Projecting my story
Onto someone else justified my actions.
Took a stand and
Fought for peace.

Now…
They are just guys.
It is all my stuff.
Peace begins within me.
When each of us chooses to be in peace
Then we will all know peace.
How does life get any better than this?

Before…
There was drama mama and
The drama dude.

Now…
Who does this belong to?
The peaceful feelings return.

Before…
Planning my life was important.
Writing down goals and
Visions kept me focused.
When I reached a goal
I felt like I got it.
Keeping an eye on the future
Gave me the road map.
The expectations limited the outcomes.

Now…
Expectations set up disappointment.
Goals and visions are limiting.
Focus on the actions and
Stay out of outcome
Allows amazing results.
Creating life in the present is a gift.
God has a more expanded vision for the future
God's paradigm is infinite.

Before…
Looked for all the answers.
Asked why.

Now…
Ask who, how,
What or where?
Attracts phenomenal results with ease.
What are the infinite possibilities?

Before…
Being in a relationship
Meant I was whole,
Life complete.

Now…
Being in relationship with me,
And God,
How does it get any better than this?
This created the space for Jim.
He nourishes my soul.
We are committed to a life that is continually growing
and expanding awareness of us, our relationship with
each other and family.

Before…
LOVE is a gift to give and receive.

Now…
We are all LOVE,
Just BE.
All of Life Comes to Us with Ease and
Joy and Glory.
That is just my interesting point of view.

Thank you for the privilege and honor for sharing *The Most Important Conversation Is the One You're Not Having.* What are the infinite possibilities that using these principles and concepts can expand your life with ease as they have others from many points on the globe? I hope they too can make a difference in your life.

If you choose to live in the question, it will free you to experience all of life with ease and joy and glory. You too will feel the grace. Now that is just another interesting point of view.

What would happen if every person in your organization and in your family interacted and spoke with the art of candor?

That simple question creates a picture for me with no boundaries. I see no limitations, vitality and masses of creativity.

I see people willing to expand and be equally fulfilled. They are doing what they love to do.

They know they are making a difference. Everyone feels listened to and appreciated.

It takes diligence and brutal honesty to be totally candid with you first, than with each other.

It all begins with you.

Blessings for you and your family,
Susan E. Greene
Houston, Texas
March 2003

Rapid Recall

> ➤ We have explored different concepts as you practiced candor as an art.

> ➤ How will you use the information and techniques in this book?

> ➤ What steps are you willing to take, starting now, to put this experience into action?

> ➤ Write a note to yourself about how you are going to use this information. Put it in an envelope.

> ➤ Open it in 30 days. Have you consistently used these tools effectively?

Notes

Introducing Susan Greene

PBS-Houston Public Television calls Susan Greene the Communication Expert. PBS aired 50 segments of *Working Relationships with Susan Greene* a call-in TV talk show. According to a PBS special on Susan, the entrepreneur, she followed her dream when she created The Corporate Renewal Center in Round Top, Texas where she takes executives on retreat.

Dr. Kathryn Kotrla, head of psychiatry at Baylor College of Medicine, a guest on Greene's latest PBS production: "Brain At Work," endorsed Susan's tool, Report Report Report as a quick and effective way to gain control of your emotions. It's now available on video.

At the request of The Executive Committee Worldwide (TEC), Greene has coached over 600 CEOs internationally in roundtables of 8-17 participants how to confront each other on their very tough issues in a non-threatening way that deepens relationships.

CEO, Drew Morris challenged Greene, "Thank you! Much better, deeper conversations. You've got something there. How are you going to fill up the whole world with it?" She took that challenge and wrote her first book and e-book, *The Most Important Conversation Is the One You're Not Having*, available at http://communicatingworks.com.

In 1986, Susan Greene founded Greene Alliances, Inc.

Her many rolls include being catalyst, mother, wife and friend. She is recognized as an international master facilitator, author, speaker, executive coach, TV personality, consultant, and mediator.

Greene's 27 years of international work spans 15 countries on five continents. Her career started at ITT where she was the recipient of ITT's "Marketing Tool of the Year" award in 1974 for Europe, Middle East and Africa, while she was director of marketing & sales for the London Sheraton Hotel. She developed a team that achieved $22 million in sales the first year of operation working with organizations globally.

Greene later returned to the U.S. and joined Boise Cascade Corporation where she increased sales by over $7 million dollars within 18 months. She expanded the product distribution by utilizing her relationship skills to set up strategic alliances with customers and vendors throughout the U.S. During her second year she successfully negotiated the industry's first long-term contract with a major oil company.

As she began working with organizations on communications, the University of Houston invited her to join them as an Adjunct Professor for continuing education. She developed a series of courses on self-directed work teams, managing conflict and communicating for accountability.

As an astute observer of human behavior, Greene's work is constantly evolving and she is now a certified International Facilitator with Access. New programs and products are available through her site: http://communicatingworks.com.

Greene learned from her mother the value of serving your community. Susan has donated her gifts and time working with the youth through Rotary. Rotary International bestowed her with a Paul Harris Fellow.

Susan and her son, Sam, expanded their lives when she married Jim Bryant in 2002. Together they enjoy four children and seven grandchildren. How did they get to be so blessed?

For More Information

What are the infinite possibilities for *you* and *your* organization to commit to continually expanding and growing profits with ease?

We invite you to contact us about our Executive & Board Retreats, Anger Management, Seminars, Couples Coaching and Personal Coaching in our offices or via the telephone.

Explore the Access classes, workshops as well as personal and weekly group sessions.

New products are being developed as we expand. How can we serve you?

Greene Alliances, Inc.
The Corporate Renewal Center
Houston, Texas
http://communicatingworks.com
catalyst@communicatingworks.com
713-782-2212

Notes

Notes

Notes

To order additional signed copies of
The Most Important Conversation
Is the One You're Not Having

Name_____

Address_____

City_____ State_____ Zip_____

copies _____ x $15.00/copy   _____

Sales tax
(TX residents please add 8.25% state sales tax.)   _____

Shipping and handling $5.00/per copy   _____

Total Amount Due   _____

Please ask about customized book covers with your personalized
message for clients or employees.
Minimum order is 100 books.

Make all checks payable to:
Greene Alliances, Inc.
The Corporate Renewal Center
1308 Chardonnay
Houston, Texas 77077-3102
713.782.2212
http://communicatingworks.com

CPSIA information can be obtained at www.ICGtesting.com
Printed in the USA
BVOW02s1050280116

434557BV00001B/37/P